THE CHARACTER OF CHRIST

THE CHARACTER
OF CHRIST

*The Fruit of the Spirit in
the Life of Our Saviour*

Jonathan Landry Cruse

THE BANNER OF TRUTH TRUST

THE BANNER OF TRUTH TRUST

Head Office
3 Murrayfield Road
Edinburgh, EH12 6EL
UK

North America Office
610 Alexander Spring Road
Carlisle, PA 17015
USA

banneroftruth.org

© Jonathan Landry Cruse 2023
First published 2023

*

ISBN
Print: 978 1 80040 332 1
Epub: 978 1 80040 333 8
Kindle: 978 1 80040 334 5

*

Typeset in 11/14 Adobe Garamond Pro
at The Banner of Truth Trust, Edinburgh

Printed in Poland
by Arka, Cieszyn

To Bryce

a kind man like his Saviour

—

And to him who has sent the Helper,

the Spirit of truth (John 15:25)

CONTENTS

ACKNOWLEDGEMENTS

A s with any project years in the making, what you have in your hands is the product of many labourers, not just the one who has his name on the cover. I would like to express my thanks, first of all, to my supportive congregation, who heard this material in sermon form during the summer of 2020. In God's providence, a series on godly virtue, planned long before the Covid-19 pandemic swept across the world, proved to be a helpful corrective to our often proud, anxious, or irritable responses to a post-lockdown world.

I give praise to God for a wife and children who help me live out a Christ-focused life. Thank you, Kerri Ann and kids, for always supporting my writing endeavours!

My ministerial colleagues, Lowell Ivey and Jeremiah Montgomery, reviewed the manuscript in the early stages and gave helpful feedback and encouragement, as did John Fesko. To him, I am particularly grateful that he cared more about me cultivating the fruit of the Spirit in my life than writing about them. A faithful friend, indeed. Jon Payne was an invaluable source of help. Ian Hamilton received a very rough draft with enthusiasm and championed its publication. To him and to all the staff of The Banner of Truth Trust I express my humble thanks, and, in particular, to my copy editor Dayspring MacLeod. Hers is a rare gift: she made editing fun.

My father-in-law, Bryce Bartruff, heard these sermons via livestream when they were first preached and would often text me that I needed to turn them into a book. When the time came, he was in the hospital fighting cancer. I would send him chapters of this book to read as I worked on it, in the hope of encouraging him while he lay in bed, waiting for or recovering from surgery. But the encouragement was all mine: even through the painful trial of disease—which included what seemed like countless setbacks—he continued to display the character of Christ. There are no better words to describe Bryce than those we find in Galatians 5:22, 23. I am grateful in particular for the joy and kindness that he brings to our family. As a token of my admiration, to you, Bryce, I dedicate this book.

Jonathan Landry Cruse
November, 2022

INTRODUCTION:

THIS IS NOT A HOW-TO BOOK

THE fruit of the Spirit as listed by the Apostle Paul in Galatians 5:22, 23 is a mainstay of Christian teaching and discipleship. Many believers memorize this grouping of virtues from an early age: love, joy, peace, patience, kindness, goodness, faithfulness, gentleness, and self-control. Ancient philosophers often compiled sets of virtues that, if embodied, would lead to the good life. But no such list exceeds the comprehensiveness or can match the sublime beauty of what is expressed here by the inspired pen of Paul. The Christian church has rightly acknowledged that those who have been born again and live in obedience to God will evince these characteristics in their lives.

But have we perhaps missed the greater point, the greater meaning, of this portion of Scripture?

The fruit of the Spirit is not a to-do list, though that is often the way Christians interpret these verses. Our autopilot approach to this text is to assume that Paul is telling us who we need to be and how we need to perform. That is a spiritually torturous way to apply this text. I don't know about you, but I consistently fail to live up to the high standard of these virtues.

Okay, I was just being polite: I *do* know about you. You're in the same boat as me. And if our relationship with God in some way is based upon our performance in this area, things are not looking good.

I think many evangelicals know this intellectually, but practically we live as though our standing with God depends on our behaviour. We need to understand that this is a list of things that are done for us and in us *by* the Spirit. When we truly possess the Spirit of God, we will possess his graces as well. That is just one of the many reasons that Paul calls this list the 'fruit of the Spirit,' as opposed to the 'accomplishments of the Christian.'

Recall that this chapter of Galatians actually includes two lists: one of vices and one of virtues. We learn a lot about the nature of the fruit of the Spirit by contrasting it with the teaching on the 'works of the flesh' in verses 19-21. 'Now the works of the flesh are evident: sexual immorality, impurity, sensuality, idolatry, sorcery, enmity, strife, jealousy, fits of anger, rivalries, dissensions, divisions, envy, drunkenness, orgies, and things like these.' That term 'works' reminds us of the legalistic trouble that we can all fall into. Works cannot bring us into the kingdom of God. 'I warn you …,' Paul writes, 'those who do such things will not inherit the kingdom of God' (verse 21).

Since *doing* evil things won't get us into the kingdom, our natural tendency would be to ask, 'What *do* I need to *do* then?' But that is to miss the point. This verse says that the kingdom is something people 'inherit'; it is a gift. Only God can bring us into his kingdom. And so, contrasted to works of the flesh—works which can never earn heaven—we have 'fruit.' Not our fruit, but the fruit of the Spirit. These graces are produced by the work of the Holy Spirit, not by our exertion or effort. This is one reason why the Spirit is so frequently referred to as God's gift throughout the New Testament (e.g., Acts 2:38; 8:20; 10:45; 11:17; 1 Cor. 12:1; Heb. 6:4).

Another point of contrast is that the previous list is described in the plural: the 'works' of the flesh. The plurality there reminds us of the competing desires of our sin. They are not a team. There is division in the works of the flesh, just as literal 'divisions' make it onto the list. On the other hand, Paul uses the singular 'fruit,' not 'fruits,' to describe the work of the Holy Spirit. It is a collective singular, which shows that there is harmony in these virtues; there is a peace amongst them, just as 'peace' is on the roster. One pastor has said to think of the fruit of the Spirit not as nine separate jewels, but rather as nine separate facets or sides on one single shimmering diamond. They belong to the one Spirit. When we receive that one Spirit we receive his fruit.

Biblical and Christological Background

God has always been after one who would bear fruit for him. Ever since the very beginning, this is what he has wanted from his image-bearers. He began with Adam, who was put in a garden to tend and keep it—to bear and cultivate fruit. It was a physical task that certainly mirrored a spiritual responsibility: to mimic in his heart and life the character of his God. But Adam sinned. In that sin was the seed of every one of those vices mentioned above.

Who would cultivate God's heavenly character on earth now? Who would be a proper image-bearer? Who would take up the role and responsibility of God's representative on earth? Would it be the nation of Israel? No, they failed also. Listen to God's indictment against them in Isaiah 5:1-7.

> Let me sing for my beloved my love song concerning his vineyard: My beloved had a vineyard on a very fertile hill. He dug it and cleared it of stones, and planted it with choice vines; he built a watchtower in the midst of it, and hewed out a wine vat in it; and he looked for it to yield grapes, but it yielded wild grapes. And now, O inhabitants of Jerusalem and men of Judah, judge between me and my vineyard. What more was there to do for my vineyard, that I have not done in it? When I looked for it to yield grapes, why did it yield wild grapes? And now I will tell you what I will do to my vineyard. I will remove its hedge, and it shall be devoured; I will break down its wall, and it

shall be trampled down. I will make it a waste; it shall not be pruned or hoed, and briers and thorns shall grow up; I will also command the clouds that they rain no rain upon it. For the vineyard of the LORD of hosts is the house of Israel, and the men of Judah are his pleasant planting; and he looked for justice, but behold, bloodshed; for righteousness, but behold, an outcry!

Israel also fails to produce the spiritual fruit that God is looking for. But a few chapters later, Isaiah makes a hopeful prophecy: there will come a Fruit-Bearer. 'There shall come forth a shoot from the stump of Jesse, and a branch from his roots shall bear fruit.' Immediately, Isaiah connects this fruit-bearing with the work of the Holy Spirit: 'And the Spirit of the LORD shall rest upon him, the Spirit of wisdom and understanding, the Spirit of counsel and might, the Spirit of knowledge and the fear of the LORD. And his delight shall be in the fear of the LORD' (Isa. 11:1-3a).[1]

This is none other than Jesus Christ. He is the descendant of Jesse and David who bears fruit for God by the power of the Holy Spirit. Jesus says regarding his ministry, 'The Spirit of the Lord is upon me, because he has anointed me to proclaim good news to the poor' (Luke 4:18, quoting Isa. 61:1). Through his Spirit-anointed

---

[1] For a fuller examination of the Old Testament background of Galatians 5:19-25, see J. V. Fesko, *The Fruit of the Spirit Is …* (Darlington: EP Books, 2011), pp. 37-48.

ministry, Christ is the One who has put an end to all vice and has paved a way for real virtue.

Therefore there is really no better way to study these gifts and graces of the Spirit than to study Jesus himself. He is the One who was endowed with the Holy Spirit of God, whose every step was in harmony with that Spirit. The Scriptures won't allow us to consider Christ without coming to terms with his Spirit. Most immediately, we meet with the fact that the incarnation was specifically a work of the Holy Spirit (Luke 1:35). This, according to the great Puritan theologian John Owen, lays the foundation for the holiness in the entirety of Christ's life. He writes,

> But the body of Christ being formed pure and exact by the Holy Ghost, there was no disposition or tendency in his constitution to the least deviation from perfect holiness in any kind. The exquisite harmony of his natural temperature made love, meekness, gentleness, patience, benignity, and goodness natural and cognate to him.[2]

While the incarnation was the foundational work, the Spirit did not leave the Saviour in the womb—he was his lifelong and constant companion. Jesus was anointed for ministry by the Spirit (Matt. 3:16), preserved through temptation by the Spirit (Luke 4:1), preached the gospel in the Spirit (Luke 4:14, 15), offered up his life through the Spirit (Heb. 9:14), and has been ushered into resur-

---

[2] John Owen, *The Works of John Owen* (Edinburgh: Banner of Truth Trust, 2018), 3:167.

rection glories by the Spirit (Rom. 8:11). And everywhere else in between, the Gospels attest that in his life and ministry the fruit of this Spirit is perfectly cultivated, grown, and manifested.

If we really want to know what it means to be loving, or have patience, or show acts of kindness, we look to the life of the Son of God. There are of course other ways to study this list. We could do word studies, or explore what other New Testament epistles instruct about these virtues, and indeed we will do some of that. But I think, and I hope, the most captivating way will be to get absorbed in what the New Testament authors had to say about Jesus himself. Truly, it is only by seeing what God has done for us in Christ that we could ever begin to live a life of meaningful obedience. If our religion is not fuelled by humility, security, and gratitude, it will by default be fuelled by things like pride, fear, and desperation. Keeping our eyes on Jesus protects us from that.

And so this study is looking at the Spirit, yes, but we are looking at the Spirit *in the life of Christ*. This is the biblical model, after all, as the Spirit's primary purpose is not to bring attention to himself but instead reveal to us in greater clarity the nature of the Son (John 14:26). Puritan George Swinnock encourages us that with the Spirit as our guide, such a study of the nature and glory of Christ will never be in vain:

> To know God affectionately, as our chiefest good, so as to give him our superlative esteem, and intensest love,

is spiritual life here, in the habit or principle, as also in the act and exercise of it; and it is the beginning, seed, preparation, and way of our eternal life hereafter. But who can know that being which infinitely passeth all knowledge? … I question whether, if I had a tongue to speak of him after that manner, ye had ears to hear of him, or hearts to understand what I should speak. But though I am not able to speak, nor you to hear of God, according to his perfection, yet through the assistance of the Holy Ghost so much may be spoken and heard of him, as may tend to our present sanctification and future salvation.[3]

His Spirit, Our Spirit

One of the glorious twists of God's story of redemption is that the Spirit of Christ becomes *our* Spirit. Jesus has not kept his companion to himself, but has generously poured out the Spirit upon his people (Luke 24:49; John 14:26). Sinclair Ferguson has remarked, 'Our Lord Jesus Christ became the Bearer of the Spirit, in order to be the Bestower of the Spirit.'[4] That means it is a fact that the work of Christ will be worked in us, not by our striving but by God's grace. Don't forget that, dear Christian.

As we reflect on these familiar words in Galatians 5, consider that they are not God's *demand* upon you

[3] George Swinnock, 'The Incomparableness of God' in *The Works of George Swinnock* (Edinburgh: Banner of Truth Trust, 1992), 4:382.

[4] Sinclair B. Ferguson, 'John Owen on the Spirit in the Life of Christ', 1 April 2001, banneroftruth.org/us/resources/articles/2001/john-owen-on-the-spirit-in-the-life-of-christ/.

so much as they are his *declaration* to you in Christ. So Paul says at the end of this list that 'those who belong to Christ Jesus *have* crucified the flesh with its passions and desires' (verse 24, emphasis added). The Son of God has put an end to the sin that would separate us from God. And by his Spirit we *can* and *will* bear fruit, the very fruit God has been looking for all along in his children.

Since the fruit of the Spirit is not a to-do list, this is not a how-to book. This is a he-did book. This is a he-is book. This is a book about the sheer unmatched beautiful character of Christ. This is a book about the person and work of our Saviour, because that is what the fruit of the Spirit is really all about. Should we be surprised that these virtues are teaching us about Christ? It is his Spirit, after all (1 Pet. 1:11)! Jesus himself told the disciples that if they have any hope of bearing 'much fruit' they must be united to him, the life-giving, fruit-producing Vine. 'Apart from me you can do nothing,' he tells them (John 15:5). Paul echoes this when he writes that 'the fruit of righteousness … comes through Jesus Christ' (Phil. 1:11).

Therefore, if we want to see the fruit of the Spirit in our lives, we must first see it in his. We must be drawn deeper into Christ in faith and love, that we may experience fuller and richer communion with him. A close examination of the character of Christ is the only thing that will change our own character.

Centuries ago, concerned that many professing believers did not actually evidence the virtues of a redeemed heart, theologian Jonathan Edwards wrote the ground-breaking treatise *Concerning Religious Affections*. Therein he writes that 'true religion, in great part, consists in holy affections.'[5] Edwards goes on to explain that by *affections* he means the actions of the will, or the way we behave based upon the disposition of our heart. Our hearts can only be properly disposed, can only have that true tenor which Paul describes in Galatians 5, if we first behold the beautiful heart of Jesus. 'The child of God,' Edwards says, 'is graciously affected, because he *sees and understands* something more of divine things than he did before, more of God or Christ, and of the glorious things exhibited in the gospel.'[6]

And so that is what we are after in this study: seeing and understanding something more of Christ, and all the wonderful glories of his gospel. To borrow from Dr Owen again, in his treatise *Meditations and Discourses on the Glory of Christ*, he makes two crucial points for why a study such as this one is so indispensable.

First, and most importantly, is because it serves eternal ends: 'It is impossible that he who never meditates with delight on the glory of Christ here in this world, who labours not to behold it by faith as it is revealed in the Scripture, should ever have any real *gracious desire* to behold it in heaven.' Indeed, Owen goes further and

---

[5] Jonathan Edwards, *A Treatise Concerning Religious Affections* in *The Works of Jonathan Edwards* (Edinburgh: Banner of Truth Trust, 1973), 1:236.

[6] Edwards, *Works*, 1:261-262, emphasis added.

links our view of Christ's glorious and beautiful character to salvation itself. 'No man shall ever behold the glory of Christ by *sight* hereafter, who doth not in some measure behold it by *faith* here in this world.'[7]

The other point Owen urges is the transformative, immediate, right-here-right-now effect of studying the character of the Saviour: 'When by faith we have attained a view of the glory of Christ … *it will be effectual unto the transformation of our souls into his image.*'[8]

There it is. Owen is telling us that if we want to change, we need to see Christ and savour all of his goodness and glory and beauty. Therefore, my hope and prayer is that in the following chapters you will come to know and adore the very fact that for you and for your salvation, Christ came down from heaven, and was love, joy, peace, patience, kindness, goodness, faithfulness, gentleness, and self-control. Now, in grateful obedience, you may be these things for him.

[7] Owen, *Works*, 1:288.
[8] Owen, *Works*, 1:321, emphasis added.

I

THE LOVE OF GOD
MADE MANIFEST

WE begin with love. In one sense, this is completely expected. The Apostle John would use this one attribute to give us what is, according to John Stott, 'the most comprehensive and sublime of all biblical affirmations about God's being'—God is love (1 John 4:8).[1] Similarly, writing in 1909, Robert Law would say that this phrase is 'the summit of all revelation.'[2]

Because love is a fitting description of God's being, it is therefore a fitting prescription for Christian behaviour, a point reinforced by essentially all of the New Testament writers. Peter says, 'Above all, keep loving one another earnestly, since love covers a multitude of sins' (1 Pet. 4:8). In Hebrews we learn that the heart of Christian ministry is '[stirring] up one another to love and good

[1] Stott, *Epistles of John* (Grand Rapids, MI: Eerdmans, 1964), p. 160.
[2] Quoted in Stott, *Epistles of John*, p. 159.

works' (10:24). According to Jude, our witness and walk will be maintained if we heed this instruction: 'keep yourselves in the love of God' (verse 21). James reminds us that in order to fulfil God's 'royal law' we must love our neighbours as ourselves (2:8)—a point which John expounds in his epistles more than any other author. 'And this is his commandment, that we believe in the name of his Son Jesus Christ and love one another, just as he has commanded us' (1 John 3:23, for just one example). In Colossians, Paul exhorts believers to 'put on' a variety of attributes that manifest themselves in outward action toward others, but he concludes, 'above all these put on love, which binds everything together in perfect harmony' (3:14). Paul would write elsewhere, when he gives the triumvirate of virtues—faith, hope, and love—that 'the greatest of these is love' (1 Cor. 13:13).

It should not come as any surprise to us that these instructions are so plentiful, or that Paul headlines the list in Galatians 5 with love. If the Spirit is sanctifying us to become more and more like the image of the invisible God, like Jesus Christ, and if somehow God's very essence can be captured in these four letters, then of course the 'greatest of these' would be love; of course that is going to kick off the list. Author Jerry Bridges wrote that 'love is the overall grace from which all others flow.'[3]

---

[3] Jerry Bridges, *The Fruitful Life* (Colorado Springs, CO: NavPress, 2006), p. 47.

Defining Love

But in our study of the fruit of the Spirit, while love is the natural place to begin, it is by no means an easy place to begin. Why? For one reason, our concept of love is so warped from the biblical conception of love. Just think about the way we use the word: I love my wife. I love my dog. I love getting a hot shower. I love pizza. I love Jesus. I love sports. I love church. I love travelling. I love my son. I love going to the lake. I love playing board games. I love being with friends.

How can this same verb be used to express my relationship to humans, God, animals, food, and hobbies? Part of the reason is that we throw the word around too much. But another reason is just the limitations of the English language. We do not linguistically distinguish between these feelings. The Greek language, on the other hand, excelled in that way, as there were three common Greek words used for the emotion of love as expressed in various contexts.[4] There is *eros*, which is romantic love. *Philia* is the love of friendship and affection. And finally there is *agape*, which is predominantly used to denote selfless, sacrificial, and unnecessary love.[5] It is unnecessary in the sense that I do not gain anything by

---

[4] In fact, many things in the aforementioned list would not even qualify for one of these words, but would simply be deemed 'pleasing'—yet further indication that we use the word 'love' too often!

[5] A few rare exceptions occur where the word is used to mean something else, as in John 3:19 or 2 Peter 2:15.

showing this love. In *eros* I sense a need for one other person. In *philia* I have a strong desire for the company and companionship of a handful of others. But in *agape* I need or desire nothing. It is the person whom I love that has the need. I see *their* need, and, simply to benefit them, not because I am going to get anything out of it, I show them love.

Of course, that is a quick and simple definition of these loves, and there will be some overlap in their use. *Agape* can at times in Scripture seem to suggest the same type of love as *philia*, the friendship love. But a distinction arises as we consider that when God commands us to love others in Scripture, which he does many times, *agape*-love is used almost exclusively. God does not command us to have a romantic partner, or close personal friends. He commands us to be sacrificial and selfless. And if we are born again by the Spirit, that love will be produced in our lives. It is this *agape*-love that stands at the start of this list in Galatians 5.

Discovering Love

Likewise, it is *agape*-love that is best seen in the life and ministry of Jesus Christ. If God is *agape*, and Jesus is God, than we should expect nothing less. His every thought and action is marked by this other-centredness. He is never once motivated by personal interest or selfish gain, but rather is always moved and motivated to help, heal, and care for others. This is *why* he lives: for grace, mercy, and compassion. Because this is so, it almost seems impossible to select a single scene from the life of Christ to demonstrate this particular fruit of the Spirit. Everywhere we look we are confronted with this remarkable *agape*-love.

We see it in synagogue sermons, meals with outcasts, miracles for the poor and sick. It is love that marks the tenor of his every conversation, and love that compels him on exhausting mission trips and preaching tours. His heart, overflowing with love for the loveless, draws him like a magnet to the needs of the wayward and lost. In a fascinating essay entitled 'The Emotional Life of Our Lord,' Princeton theologian B. B. Warfield points out that compassion 'is the emotion which is most frequently attributed to him.'[6] His entire life is a great exposition of this verse: 'the fruit of the Spirit is love.'

And yet, Jesus tells us where we are to look to find the most powerful display of love—and it is not in his life, but in his death. He says as much in John 15:13, 'Greater love [*agape*] has no one than this, that someone lay down his life for his friends.' There is something about the cross that shows love in a way that overshadows everything else Christ did on this earth. An old hymn acknowledges that 'we read [the love of God] best in him who came bearing for us the cross of shame.'[7] That is what Jesus is teaching

---

[6] B. B. Warfield, *The Person and Work of Christ* (Phillipsburg, NJ: P&R Publishing, 1950), p. 96.

[7] Horatius Bonar, 'O Love of God, How Strong and True', 1861.

in John 15:13. It is as though he says, 'If you want to know love best, learn about what it means to lay down your life.'

This familiar verse comes in the context of wider teaching on the subject of love. Jesus and his disciples have partaken of the Passover, and he is about to be handed over to the Jewish council and be put on trial. Betrayal and death are nigh, which gives these few chapters (13-16) particular import—it is Jesus' final discourse, his last instructions to his disciples before his death. And what does Jesus want to impress upon his disciples in this significant moment? The importance of love.

In Jesus' final sermon, *agape* is on his lips nearly thirty times. He speaks of his love for his disciples, and his Father's love for him, and therefore his Father's love for the disciples. But most particularly he emphasizes their need to display love to one another: 'A new commandment I give to you, that you love one another: just as I have loved you, you also are to love one another. By this all people will know that you are my disciples, if you have love for one another' (13:34, 35; cf. 15:12). Interestingly, the other great theme that Christ returns to over and again in these chapters is the coming of the Holy Spirit, who will empower and enable the disciples to keep his commands—laying the foundation for Paul's teaching that true love must be a fruit of the Holy Spirit in our lives.

When the disciples hear that they are commanded to love, what question do you think comes into their heads? The very one that comes into ours when we are given the same command. *What does that love look like?* Jesus antici-pates their question in 15:13 when he says, 'Greater love has no one than this, that one lay down his life for his friends.' That is likely not the answer they were hoping for, and the same can be said of us. We would much rather that Jesus had commanded a love that could be fulfilled simply by helping your friend move, or picking them up at the airport. A love that is just a *little* inconvenient. We could handle that, and we would feel pretty good about ourselves, too. But that is not the love Jesus taught or displayed. John will not let us get away from this point, as he brings it up again in his first epistle: 'By this we know love, that he laid down his life for us, and we ought to lay down our lives for the brothers' (1 John 3:16).

When we look to the cross, the premier display of *agape*-love in the life of Christ and in the history of the entire universe, what do we see? What do we learn about love? We will spend all eternity discovering the answer to that question. But right now our question is more narrow: when looking to the cross, what can we discover about the very love that will be worked out in our lives as we manifest the Holy Spirit's presence and power? For now, let us explore four brief answers to that massive and marvellous question.

Jesus' love is willing and ready

When a friend and I were embarking on a project to add a bathroom in my basement, one of the necessary steps was knocking down space for a door in an eight-inch-thick concrete wall. We were building the thing from scratch, so there were plenty of other steps that needed to be completed: plumbing, framing, tiling, drywalling, and running electric cables. This doorway was the most foreboding, however, and so we kept avoiding it. We left it until the very end, which actually made the process a whole lot harder, since we had to be sure not to damage any of the finished construction surrounding it. Knowing that it would be difficult made us drag our feet in approaching it.

And yet we find the exact opposite in the cross. Knowing the difficulty that would face him at Calvary did not slow Jesus down. Throughout his public ministry he had his face set like a flint to the cross. He knew full well that the great crescendo of his mission would be his own anguished cry of death, and yet he was still determined to reach that end. Why? How? Love is the explanation. It was a love for sinners destined for hell that would spur him on towards the goal. If we think the cross is only a miscarriage of justice—that is, only a result of a friend's betrayal, a mob's rage, and a governor's spinelessness—then it would almost seem as though Jesus' death was involuntary. But the picture that the Gospels paint leading up to the crucifixion says something quite different. Luke 9:51, 'When the days drew near for him to be taken up, he set his face to go to Jerusalem.' Jesus was *resolved* to die. He was willing and ready. He did not drag his feet, though it would be unpleasant. Why? Because of *love*. Craig Troxel writes:

> In the end the Father gave Jesus what he wanted, to hand over his own spirit for us in love (John 19:30; Gal. 2:20; Eph. 5:2). His life was not taken from him; Christ laid down his life of his own accord (Luke 9:51; John 10:18; Phil. 2:8). This is love. It is love that flows from an undivided heart. It is dedicated to a singular purpose. *There is nothing more sure or more pure than this love.*[8]

Are we ready to love? Or do we drag our feet? We are commanded to love, yes, but if we only love in response to a command, that is not the fruit of the Spirit, nor what God is after. God is glorified when we have a disposition of love within us at all times, ready to express itself the moment the opportunity arises. Nineteenth-century Reformed minister George Bethune writes that in the context of this list, love means 'not so much the acting or going forth of love, as that *loving temper*, or *lovingness of soul*, which disposes us to love whenever the proper object is presented.'[9] When we look at the life of Christ, we see that is exactly how he loved. It was who he was— even to his final breath.

---

[8] A. Craig Troxel, *With All Your Heart: Orienting Your Mind, Desires, and Will Toward Christ* (Wheaton, IL: Crossway, 2020), p. 106, emphasis added.

[9] George Bethune, *The Fruits of the Spirit* (Philadelphia: Mentz & Rovoudt, 1845), p. 44.

Jesus' love is sacrificial

At the cross, we learn that real love is marked by sacrifice. It does not close up shop and head home at the first sight of inconvenience—rather, it thrives on inconvenience. The love of the cross is magnified by the pains that Jesus bore there. The bleeding, the thirst, the humiliation, and the wounds all join together as Christ's stunning pronouncement of 'I love you' to a sinful world.

This is the main thrust of Jesus' line in the Upper Room: laying down one's life is the language of sacrifice. Of course, 'life' is more than a series of heartbeats—our passions and pursuits and preferences all make up our life. Insofar as we sacrifice our time, money, wants, and preferences for the benefit of others, we should rest assured that we are living in obedience to this instruction.

But let us not lose sight of the punch of Jesus' claim, or the power of the cross: the greatest display of love is in laying down one's literal life. It was by and through the Holy Spirit that Christ loved in this sacrificial way (Heb. 9:14), and thus a fruit of that same Spirit in our lives will be sacrifice—even the *ultimate* sacrifice. John does not wish us to water down the extent of God's command to love, and so he puts it as bluntly as this: 'By this we know love, that he laid down his life for us, and we ought to lay down our lives for the brothers' (1 John 3:16). The import of this verse is one that we would do well to sit with and meditate over.

Jesus wants us to get to the place where we see that living is not the most important part of life. Actually, as a Christian, the most important part of my life is *other* people's living and welfare (Phil. 2:3). Whatever I can do to enhance that, protect that, or help that is love, and that is what I am called to—even if it means dying to do so.

Jesus' love is gracious

Graciousness is the key attribute of gift-giving. It is the desire to bestow kindnesses upon people simply because there is such joy in the act of giving. *Agape*-love is a love that gives. It's a love that wants, above all else, to benefit the recipient. In the words of one writer, 'It is the nature of God's love to give, just as it is the nature of the sun to shine.'[10] The most well-known verse on love in all of Scripture is connected with the act of giving: 'For God so loved the world that he gave his only Son' (John 3:16). That gift was opened for us at the cross. Christ went to death in order that we would receive 'the free gift of God [which] is eternal life' (Rom. 6:23).

Recognizing this staggering gift we have been given is the only thing that can enable us to love in such gracious and sacrificial ways. We have seen that God may well be calling us to display love in the act of laying down our lives, which is a very difficult teaching to swallow. But it is the death of Christ that gives us the courage to step

---

[10] David Jackman, *The Message of John's Letters* (Downers Grove, IL: InterVarsity Press, 1988), p. 100.

out of ourselves and live and love in this way, because through his loving death he gave us immortality (2 Tim. 1:10). We do not need to be afraid if the act of love carries us to the threshold of death—because we know there is eternal life for us on the other side.

The life and death of Baptist minister John Harper is a fitting example of how the gospel enables one to love in amazing ways. In 1912, Mr Harper and his daughter were heading from Scotland to America aboard the RMS *Titanic* for a preaching engagement at Moody Church in Chicago. Once the ship hit the iceberg and began to go down, and after getting his daughter into a lifeboat, Harper stayed back to give the masses one last chance to know Christ. In the frigid water he swam from person to person, pleading with them to believe on the Lord Jesus. Rebuffed by a certain man at the offer of salvation, he promptly gave him his own life vest (the greatest gift that man had ever received, no doubt) and said, 'You need this more than I do.'

Jesus' love is merciful
The love that the Spirit of God creates and cultivates in our hearts reflects the divine display of love at the cross in at least one more way: it is merciful. Notice a slight nuance from the previous point: love is gracious in that it gives, but love is merciful in that *it gives to people who do not deserve it*. Indeed, his love is for people who only deserve punishment and enmity.

Jesus had said that the greatest love is to lay one's life down for one's friends. At the cross he ups his own ante. His love is greater than the greatest love, because he lays his life down for his enemies. Paul revels in this truth in Romans 5: 'For while we were still weak, at the right time Christ died for the ungodly. For one will scarcely die for a righteous person—though perhaps for a good person one would dare even to die—but God shows his love for us in that while we were still sinners, Christ died for us' (verses 6-8).

Consider whom you choose to show love towards, and the occasions you choose to show it. Do you internally calculate whether or not someone is worth your time or attention? Do you consider what you might get out of a particular act of generosity or compassion? *Agape*-love is not part of a you-scratch-my-back-I'll-scratch-yours exchange. When notions of 'deserving' and 'undeserving' factor into our relationship with others, we are actually fighting against the fruit that the Spirit is cultivating in our hearts. That is not the love the Spirit produces, because it is not the love that Jesus showed to us. The words of Isaac Watts beautifully capture this love of Christ toward sinners like me and you, who are far more deserving of his wrath and judgment than of his loving favour:

> Alas and did my Saviour bleed,
>> And did my Sovereign die?
> Would he devote that sacred head
>> For such a worm as I?

> Was it for crimes that I had done
> He groaned upon the tree?
> Amazing pity, grace unknown,
> And love beyond degree.[11]

Desiring Love

There is an innate desire in all of us to know love and to be loved. God made us that way. Unbeknownst to them, The Beatles were on to something unexpectedly biblical with their famous line, 'All you need is love.' That is so profoundly true. And our world desperately needs it. You and I desperately need it. But what kind of love do we need? *Eros* or *philia* can never fulfil this desire. Sex or friendship will never fill the heart's deepest longing. We need *agape*. Everyone seeks to be completely known, flaws, faults, and all, and still loved and wanted anyway.

Even so, *agape*-love on a mere human plane will never be enough. It is never strong enough. I think of the four years I lived in downtown Philadelphia and encountered homelessness at every turn: my heart was so cold to the need, my affections so tepid and weak. The conditions of the poor would capture the full force of our Saviour's love, and yet I had become calloused and often averted my gaze to people's needs. But even when we do step out of ourselves and show compassion in a willing, sacrificial, grace-filled, and merciful way, it still cannot reach the depths of the needs of the human condition. That

[11] Isaac Watts, 'Alas, And Did My Saviour Bleed', 1707.

is because at bottom what we really need is forgiveness, salvation, and fellowship with God.

And so the real desire of the human heart is not just love, nor is it even *agape*-love—it is the love of Jesus Christ. Without Jesus, real love is impossible. Without Jesus, our testimony can only be that we are 'hated by others and hating one another' (Titus 3:3). Without Jesus, 'all you need is love' is a meaningless mantra. But with Jesus it is the message of the gospel—because it is his love that truly covers a multitude of sins and saves us from hell. When we have received that love, we are able to release it back into the world. The love that comes from the Spirit is a cruciform love: a love that is literally shaped by the cross. We will love in such a way that people will see Christ through it. With Paul, our testimony will become lives lived 'by faith in the Son of God, who *loved* me and gave himself for me' (Gal. 2:20, emphasis added).

Such love dissolves the heart in thankfulness. It melts the eyes to tears. But the fitting response is to go back into the world and give our lives to the mission of displaying this very love:

> But drops of grief can ne'er repay
>   the debt of love I owe.
> Here, Lord, I give myself away:
>   'tis all that I can do.[12]

---

[12] Watts, 'Alas, And Did My Saviour Bleed'.

THE JOY OF YOUR MASTER

D o you think of Jesus as being a *happy* person? Does a joyful Jesus seem incongruous to you? After all, dealing with sin is serious business—maybe Jesus never had time to enjoy himself. We know he was 'a man of sorrows, acquainted well with grief'—was he acquainted well with gladness? We know 'Jesus wept'—did Jesus laugh, smile, or have fun? Was he *happy*?

The answer we must give to that is an enthusiastic and resounding *Yes!*

The Embodiment of Joy
Not only was Jesus happy, but he was the happiest man who ever lived. John Piper says that Jesus 'is, and always will be, indestructibly happy.'[1] *Happy* has become too weak a word in today's parlance, so note that we mean

---

[1] John Piper, *Seeing and Savoring Jesus Christ* (Wheaton, IL: Crossway, 2004), pp. 35-36.

a deep and abiding pleasure and contentment. If that sounds strange to us, then we need to rethink our perceptions of the Saviour. He is the very incarnation of joy!

There is anecdotal evidence in the gospels that Jesus was filled with joy and gladness. For one thing, it was not uncommon to find Jesus at parties and festivals. He enjoyed them so much that he was liable to the charge of gluttony and drunkenness—a charge unlikely to be levelled against a curmudgeon (Luke 7:34)! People of his day were not used to rabbis who could take God's word seriously and somehow also enjoy fun and fellowship. Likewise, in his role as rabbi, it was not beyond Jesus to use irony and wit in his teachings (e.g., Matt. 23:24). Also, there is the fact that children were drawn to him and he to them. It takes the spark of joy to enter the world of children.

Beyond this anecdotal evidence, there are numerous places in Scripture where the characteristic of joy is ascribed to Christ. In the parable of the talents, it is his joy that the good and faithful servants will enter into upon completion of their labours (Matt. 25:21). Through the parable of the hidden treasure Jesus describes his joy in redeeming the elect as being like a man who finds a buried treasure in a field, and with great excitement and gladness sells all he has to purchase the field and claim its treasure. In other words, it is with joy that he comes to do the work of redemption. This is spelled out even more clearly in Hebrews 12:2, which tells us it was for 'the joy that was set before him' that he could endure the cross. Jesus is the shepherd who 'rejoices' at finding one lost and straying sheep (Matt. 18:13).

It is quite astounding that we so rarely think of Jesus as joyful when the very first sermon ever preached in the New Testament church highlighted this very fact. It was Peter's Pentecost sermon, where he interprets the words of Psalm 16 as being truly spoken by and fulfilled in Christ: 'For David says concerning him [that is, Christ], "I saw the Lord always before me, for he is at my right hand that I may not be shaken; therefore my heart was glad, and my tongue rejoiced; my flesh also will dwell in hope. For you will not abandon my soul to Hades, or let your Holy One see corruption. You have made known to me the paths of life; you will make me full of gladness with your presence"' (Acts 2:25-28). Think about that: Peter's very first sermon includes a sub-point on the joy of Jesus!

Similarly, Hebrews 1:9 quotes Psalm 45, telling us that these very words are spoken by the Father *about* the Son: 'You have loved righteousness and hated wickedness; therefore God, your God, has anointed you with the oil of gladness beyond your companions.' Did you catch that? God has anointed his Son with gladness *beyond* that of his friends. Because he has followed and loved and obeyed the Lord with all that is in him, he has been given a measure of happiness that is over and above anyone else on earth. Again, Piper says, 'Jesus Christ is the happiest being in the universe. His gladness is greater than all the angelic gladness of heaven. He mirrors perfectly the infinite, holy, indomitable mirth of his Father … [He is] glad with the very gladness of God.'[2]

Perhaps you are thinking, 'Okay. So what? Why does it matter that Jesus was joyful?' It matters because it informs our understanding of what it means to be a Christian, of what it looks like to grow in Christ-likeness. If we have the Spirit of Christ, and if he is producing fruit for Christ in our hearts, it will come with this very joy. We are being re-created to reflect the character of Christ, and Christ was joyful.

In John 15:11, Jesus says to his disciples, 'These things I have spoken to you, that my joy may be in you, and that your joy may be full.' We reach the pinnacle of happiness and joy when we fully receive who Jesus is and what he taught. When his joy is in us, that is when we are the most joyful. Our union to the joyful Vine is vital in order to bear that same fruit in our lives (John 15:4). But if we think Jesus is devoid of happiness and gladness, this cannot happen. If we have an inaccurate, and therefore incomplete, picture of who Christ is, then we will have an incomplete joy.

Some Christians have taken a very austere and serious approach to expressing their faith—and there are certainly good reasons to be cautious of a glib approach. But at times we can over-correct, and lose the joy that

---

[2] Piper, *Seeing and Savoring*, pp. 36, 37.

is Jesus. We tragically conclude that Jesus and joy are like East and West, and 'never the twain shall meet.' We make the fatal flaw of concluding that Jesus is actually a killjoy, not joy incarnate. He is the embodiment of all godly gladness. No one can truly have Christ in their hearts without also having his joy there, too.

The Source of Joy

There is a single instance in the Gospels where we actually are told Jesus 'rejoiced.' It is in Luke 10, immediately following a discourse Jesus has with his disciples on the source of true joy. Actually, Jesus begins by saying what we should *not* rejoice in.

> The seventy-two returned with joy, saying, 'Lord, even the demons are subject to us in your name!' And he said to them, 'I saw Satan fall like lightning from heaven. Behold, I have given you authority to tread on serpents and scorpions, and over all the power of the enemy, and nothing shall hurt you. Nevertheless, do not rejoice in this, that the spirits are subject to you, but rejoice that your names are written in heaven.' In that same hour he rejoiced in the Holy Spirit and said, 'I thank you, Father, Lord of heaven and earth, that you have hidden these things from the wise and understanding and revealed them to little children; yes, Father, for such was your gracious will. All things have been handed over to me by my Father, and no one knows who the Son is except the Father, or who the Father is except the Son and anyone to whom the Son chooses to reveal him.'—Luke 10:17-22

The context of the passage is the sending of the seventy-two disciples on the very first New Covenant missionary journey. They go two-by-two into all of the surrounding region, healing the sick, casting out demons, and preaching the message that 'the kingdom of God has come near to you' (verse 9). Upon completion of their task, the seventy-two return to Jesus 'with joy' at the success of their mission. We can almost picture them skipping back to Christ. They are elated at the power that was at their disposal, exclaiming, 'Lord, even the demons are subject to us in your name!' (verse 17). Then comes Jesus' reply: 'Do not rejoice in this, that the spirits are subject to you, but rejoice that your names are written in heaven' (verse 20).

A false source of joy

Notice first that Jesus exposes their false and faulty source of joy. In the particular context it is the fact that they had power over demons—which, if we are honest, must have been an exhilarating experience. At a broader level, though, we could say the disciples' joy was rooted in at least two things.

First, they rejoiced in their *circumstance*. It is easy to be happy when things are going well, and things were going really, really well for the disciples. They were coming back with the same rush of a soldier after victory on the battlefield. After witnessing first-hand God using them to advance his kingdom on earth, they were quite understandably on a sort of ministry high. But the challenge is to find joy even when it seems like Satan is prevailing and our circumstances are dire. It is a dangerous thing for joy to hinge upon success or failure, for then it would often be in precariously low supply.

Second, the disciples rejoice in *themselves*. Yes, they acknowledge that the demons are in subjugation to the 'name' of Christ, but you can sense what really excites them. Where does the emphasis lie in their announcement? Do they come back and report, 'Even the demons are subject to us *in your* name,' or 'Even the demons are subject *to us* in your name'? Knowing my own heart, I have a good guess.

J. C. Ryle comments, 'There was much false fire in that joy. There was evidently self-satisfaction in that report of achievement.'[3] They were quite full of themselves at this moment, and Jesus had to bring them back down and remind them that their authority and invincibility comes from his hand (verse 19). Are we never guilty of the same? In humility, let us remember that we are nothing without Christ. 'Therefore let anyone who thinks that he stands take heed lest he fall,' and his joy fall along with him (1 Cor. 10:12). Jesus 'saw how much [the disciples] were lifted up by their first victory. He wisely checks them in their undue exultation.'[4]

---

[3] J. C. Ryle, *Luke* (Edinburgh: Banner of Truth Trust, 2012), 1:273.
[4] Ryle, *Luke*, 1:273.

The true source of joy

The problem with these sources of joy is that they cannot last—so Jesus turns their attention to something that will last. He says, 'Do not rejoice in this, that the spirits are subject to you, but rejoice that your names are written in heaven.' Here we find the true source of lasting joy: it is that which is written in heaven. The verb tense here indicates something that is permanent. When we think of divine pen meeting divine paper, it is an image of all of God's unchangeable purposes throughout all of eternity (Rev. 5:1-5; 20:12). More specifically, Jesus is undoubtedly referencing 'the book of life,' which we are told in Revelation contains the names which have been written before the foundation of the world (17:8) and names that can never be erased (3:5). As Dennis Johnson says, 'It is the one book in all the universe that spells the difference between eternal life and unending death.'[5]

In the very next verse we read, '[Jesus] rejoiced in the Holy Spirit and said, "I thank you, Father, Lord of heaven and earth, that you have hidden these things from the wise and understanding and revealed them to little children; yes, Father, *for such was your gracious will.*"' Here is that single instance where Jesus is said to be rejoicing, so let us pay careful attention. What is Jesus rejoicing in? The saving of souls, undoubtedly. He is rejoicing in the work of God that was manifest through

[5] Dennis E. Johnson, *Triumph of the Lamb: A Commentary on Revelation* (Phillipsburg, NJ: P&R Publishing, 2001), p. 299.

the disciples' mission, too. He rejoices in the kingdom of God and the knowledge of God that is breaking into this world (see also verse 22). But I believe we can sum it all up simply like this: *Jesus rejoices in the will of God*. Specifically, the will of God to reveal his divine wonders, not to those of status and renown, but to the humble disciples. This is God's plan and it makes Jesus joyful.

One commentator suggests that the translation 'rejoice' is far too weak a rendering of the Greek word.[6] The word suggests an inward joy that expresses itself outwardly, through verbal exclamation and even bodily movement. It's actually a compound Greek word coming from the word for 'much' and the word for 'jump'—it's as though Jesus was leaping for joy here.

And note especially that this kind of profound exultation comes from the Holy Spirit: 'In that same hour, he rejoiced *in the Holy Spirit*,' the text says in verse 21. How fascinating in our study of the fruit of the Spirit to learn that the Spirit is present and active in this instance of our Saviour's exceeding joy! B. B. Warfield said, 'this exultation was a product in Christ—and therefore in his human nature—of the operation of the Holy Spirit, whom we must suppose to have been always working in the human soul of Christ, sustaining and strengthening it.'[7]

---

[6] Leon Morris, *The Gospel According to Luke* (Grand Rapids, MI: Eerdmans, 1988), p. 203.

[7] Warfield, *The Person and Work of Christ*, p. 123.

This is godly gladness through and through: the Holy Spirit fills Jesus with such joy at divine work and will that it can only be properly expressed in praise and thanksgiving to the almighty Father. This is what should come to mind when we think of the joy promised to us in the fruit of the Spirit.

The Permanence of Joy

So this is precisely what we are after as Christians: this kind of Jesus-joy. We want that which is produced by the Spirit and finds its source in the unchangeable and perfect plans of God, not the unstable pleasurable circumstances of life or the fleeting successes of self. The Christian is one who cannot help but exult in God for all that he does and will do. George Bethune once wrote that the Christian 'is joyful in the knowledge of God. A true ear has delight in perfect harmony. A true eye has delight in perfect proportion. So does a true and holy soul delight in God. He delights to contemplate infinite power directed by infinite wisdom.'[8]

Why is God's will worth our rejoicing? Because of what we know about it. We know that it is good and perfect (Rom. 12:2). It is informed by gracious love for sinners like us (Eph. 1:3-6). We know that it is never cruel, but is marked by divine compassion and forbearance (2 Pet. 3:9). We know that God is directing the unfolding of all of history for the good of those who love him and

---

[8] Bethune, *The Fruitful Life*, p. 67.

have been called according to his purposes (Rom. 8:28). And we know that this plan of God can never change or fail (Psa. 33:11; Isa. 40:8).

We are God's beloved children, and this is the amazing reality he has revealed to us and not to the wise and understanding people of this age. How could we do anything but rejoice when this is the window onto the world that we have been given? Joy, truly speaking, then is the property of believers. For G. K. Chesterton it is 'the gigantic secret of the Christian.'[9]

R. C. Sproul tells the story of looking at a photograph of a native tribe in Africa with whom his friend served as a missionary. His friend told him twelve of the people in the photo had been converted, and asked Sproul if he could identify which ones. Sproul said, 'There was nothing distinctive about those in the picture. They all looked and dressed the same way. Nevertheless, choosing the twelve was an easy task—they were the ones who were radiant. The joy and life of Christ was written plainly on their countenance.'[10]

The presence of joy corresponds to the presence of Christ's Spirit. Jesus himself even remarks to his disciples that the coming of the Helper will be the heaven-sent antidote to the 'sorrow [that] has filled [their] heart' (John 16:6). It is a powerful testimony to a gloomy world that we know 'the joy of [God's] salvation' (Psa. 51:12).

---

[9] G. K. Chesterton, *Orthodoxy* (New York: Doubleday, 1990), p. 160.
[10] R. C. Sproul, *Matthew* (Wheaton, IL: Crossway, 2013), p. 99.

At Buckingham Palace in London, the royal standard is flown to indicate when the sovereign is inside. The flag is clearly visible day or night so that the citizens know whether or not the monarch is residing in the palace. When the monarch resides elsewhere, the royal standard flies over that palace, home, or even yacht. In the same way, wherever we go, joy should be the banner flown over us to indicate to all that Christ the King is living within our hearts.

When the source of our joy is the perfect and permanent plan of God, our joy will be permanent, too. This is the only thing that can make sense of the numerous New Testament commands for Christians to be joyful, an instruction that is seemingly easier said than done when you consider how hard life can be. James encourages us at the outset of his epistle to 'count it all joy, my brothers, when you meet trials of various kinds' (1:2). The world which finds its source of joy in circumstances cannot make any sense of this teaching. As Christians we struggle with it, too. How can James possibly expect us to be joyful even when we are going through trials and difficulties? An understanding of God's will during those trials is the only answer. We know that God uses trials to make us more Christ-like, more dependent on him in all things. Trials make us better people, really—'perfect and complete, lacking in nothing' (verse 4). For the unbeliever, the fiery trial is nothing other than a precursor to the hellish fires of eternity, and quite understandably would suck the happiness out of the soul. But for the believer, the fiery trial is preparing us for heaven, and therefore does not consume us *or* our joy.

Likewise, Paul's instruction to us is to 'rejoice in the Lord always; again I will say, rejoice' (Phil. 4:4). He reminds us of the true source of our joy: rejoice *in the Lord*. It is only when God is our gladness that we can fulfil the hardest part of this exhortation (that 'always' bit). When we make who God is and what he is done, and is doing, our source of joy, we will feel literally exhilarated from it. Nehemiah said that 'the joy of the LORD is [our] strength' (Neh. 8:10).

Of course, the New Testament writers were not expecting Christians to always be in a good mood, so do not misunderstand. Nor are they discounting the seriousness of hardships and heartaches that we will face in this world. Remember, Jesus Christ was a 'man of sorrows'—and yet he was also a man of joy. What the Holy Spirit is producing in our hearts is the joy of the Saviour, which is a *serious* joy. A joy that can face the seriousness of life head-on and still come out on top. Nothing can overwhelm a joy that is rooted in God. This is the very joy Jesus had. As Warfield puts it, Jesus had:

> ... not the shallow joy of mere pagan delight in living, nor the delusive joy of a hope destined to failure; but the deep exultation of a conqueror setting captives free. This joy underlay all his sufferings and shed its

light along the whole thorn-beset path which was trodden by his torn feet.[11]

Dear Christian, maybe you need to be reminded that God wants you to be joyful. Go ahead, let yourself be happy. The Christian has every reason to be! Moses said the very same to Israel: 'Happy are you, O Israel! Who is like you, a people saved by the LORD?' (Deut. 33:29). We know the saving work of God. As one writer explains, the Christian turns from the world and to the gospel, and 'to [our] unutterable and indescribable delight, [we] encounter the rare and refreshing words: "It is finished!" Are there any happier words in the universe?'[12] What can shake the joy of the one who receives these words in faith?

We have seen that Christ himself was the happiest man to walk this earth, and he is in our hearts. His Spirit of joy is in us and making us more and more like him. That can only happen, then, if we become more and more joyful. Let's not allow any circumstance to prevent that in us. Nor should we let any misguided understanding of what it means to be a serious Christian keep us from joy and gladness in the Lord.

The Puritans get a bad rap nowadays. Many people think they were the original killjoys. They are immortalized in that sorry adjective used to describe strictness

---

[11] Warfield, *The Person and Work of Christ*, p. 126.
[12] David Murray, *The Happy Christian: Ten Ways to Be a Joyful Believer in a Gloomy World* (Nashville, TN: Thomas Nelson, 2015), p. 47.

and austerity and boredom: *puritanical*. And yet when pondering what it means to be a human, when considering what the entire purpose of life is, you know what the Puritans said? 'Man's chief end is to glorify God and to *enjoy him* forever.'[13]

The Place of Joy

We have asserted that to have a permanent joy, it cannot be rooted in this passing world, but rather in the unchanging and unchangeable character of God, especially as that is revealed in Christ. One Appalachian folk hymn speaks in rich theological expression of what the here and now offers us: 'No tranquil joy on earth I know, no peaceful sheltering dome: this world's a wilderness of woe, this world is not my home.'[14] If woe is the trademark of a fallen earth, joy is the trademark of heaven. Therefore, if we are to have a permanent joy, we must keep our hearts fixed upon the place where joy will be permanent: the new heavens and the new earth.

Kingdoms tend to take on the characteristics of their king. Think of how C. S. Lewis captured this for our imaginations in *The Lion, the Witch, and the Wardrobe*. When the evil White Witch rules Narnia, grey and cold cover the land, the subjects wallow under the shadow of terror, and no one dares go outside for fear of being turned to lifeless stone. Under her tyrannical reign,

[13] Westminster Shorter Catechism, Q. and A. 1 (emphasis added).
[14] Elizabeth Mills, 'O Land of Rest, For Thee I Sigh!', 1837.

Narnia is best described as 'always winter and never Christmas.'[15] And yet when the true king Aslan returns, the snow begins to melt, the rivers run and glimmer like crystal, and the White Witch's winter is destroyed. With the warmth of his breath, frozen statues are brought to life, and the world begins to again dance and rejoice as it once did when he first sang it into creation.

> Wrong will be right, when Aslan comes in sight,
> At the sound of his roar, sorrows will be no more,
> When he bares his teeth, winter meets its death
> And when he shakes his mane, we shall have spring
> again.[16]

How much more wonderful to know that Christ is the King reigning in heaven! As he is the King of joy, so too heaven will be the land of joy. The character of Christ will radiate through his kingdom and benefit and bless all who dwell there: 'He will wipe away every tear from their eyes, and death shall be no more, neither shall there be mourning, nor crying, nor pain anymore, for the former things have passed away' (Rev. 21:4). The wilderness of woe will have given way for the land of pure delight. A Puritan prayer expressed it like this:

> There is no joy like the joy of heaven, for in that state are no sad divisions, unchristian quarrels, contentions, evil designs, weariness, hunger, cold, sadness,

[15] C. S. Lewis, *The Lion, the Witch, and the Wardrobe* (New York: Collier, 1970), p. 16.
[16] Lewis, *The Lion, the Witch, and the Wardrobe*, p. 75.

sin, suffering, persecutions, toils of duty. O healthful place where none are sick! O happy land where all are kings! O holy assembly where all are priests! How free a state where none are servants except to thee! Bring me speedily to the land of joy.[17]

As we are still on this side of that reality, we can maintain our joy by continually reminding ourselves that this is our destination. In fact, more than being merely a future goal, it is our present spiritual place of residency (Col. 3:1-3). The Holy Spirit places heaven in us before he places us in heaven. He gives us the joy of heaven *now*. Yet still we long for that day when, after battling through the sorrows and travails of earth, we hear the benediction of our Saviour: 'Well done, good and faithful servant … Enter into the joy of your master' (Matt. 25:21).

[17] 'Joy' in *The Valley of Vision* (Edinburgh: Banner of Truth Trust, 2009), p. 160.

3

HE HIMSELF IS OUR PEACE

HAVE you ever considered the fact that 'peace' may just be the most important word in the Bible? I'm not just referring to simple word count here: the fact that the word 'peace' appears nearly five hundred times in Scripture. I am saying that when you take the entire story of the Bible together, it could be legitimately claimed that the main theme is really that of peace. Now, there are a lot of pretty important words and concepts in Scripture, so maybe that seems like an audacious, if not narrow-minded, assertion. But nevertheless my claim is this: God's entire purpose for the universe is best summarized with the word *peace*.

Why do I say this? Consider the beginning of all things. In the Bible's record of the making of the universe, God's creative acts are depicted as the in-breaking of peace upon a chaotic world, since 'the earth was without form and void' (Gen. 1:2). The world was pure chaos, and into that chaos God brings order, peace, *shalom*. *Shalom* is one of those sublime Hebrew words for which there is no exact English counterpart. *Peace* is probably the closest, but it also has connotations of prosperity, completion, perfection. That is the world that God made and brought his image-bearers into.

Sin fractures that *shalom*. Whereas before, all of nature was in perfect harmony, and creation in a peaceful relationship with God himself, now there is division. Is not the whole of Scripture unfolding the story of God reversing this fractured relationship between the world and himself? God's desire is that earth will reflect the *shalom* of heaven. Hinting to us that this is his plan is the rather obvious fact that heaven's outpost on earth was named Jerusalem: 'the city of peace.' Peace is his mission, and his promise to restore humanity to a right relationship with himself is called the 'covenant of peace' (Isa. 54:10). The one who fulfils that promise is 'the prince of peace' (Isa. 9:6), sent by none other than the One who is named repeatedly the 'God of peace' (Rom. 15:33; 16:20; Phil. 4:9; 1 Thess. 5:23; Heb. 13:20), and this is declared unto us in the proclamation of the 'gospel of peace' (Eph. 6:15).

And what is the culmination of God's grand purpose of peace? The great prophet Isaiah looks to the future and paints for us a beautiful picture of how it all ends: 'The wolf shall dwell with the lamb, and the leopard shall lie down with the young goat, and the calf and the lion and the fattened calf together; and a little child shall lead them' (Isa. 11:6). Does that imagery not speak to us sweetly of the perfection and blessedness of peace?

When we survey the hundreds of instances of the word 'peace' in the Bible, we begin to see there are three main types of peace of which the Bible speaks. The first is an *eternal peace*—the peace between God and mankind that begins now in the hearts of the converted and will continue on into everlasting bliss forever. This establishes a second peace, which is an *internal peace*, again in the hearts of believers, that gives them a calm and trusting inner disposition and frame of spirit no matter what may happen in life. This will then pour forth into a third and final peace—an *external peace*, or a peaceableness between man and man. This is where that fruit of the Spirit is seen most clearly: when we are able to live in harmony with our neighbours. Let us look at each in turn.

Eternal Peace

The internal and external peace depend upon the eternal peace. Or to put it another way, if we have no peace with God, we can have no peace at all. This eternal peace is what we have already been considering: God's primary plan for his entire created universe. It is his plan that we should know the prosperity and perfection of peace that, while so foreign to us, is completely natural to his own being.

And as we consider the fruit of the Spirit in the life of Christ, we need to begin by seeing that this eternal, everlasting peace between God and all things is precisely what Christ came to accomplish. He came to end our war with God. He came to bring peace and harmony to the entire cosmos. 'He himself is our peace,' Paul says (Eph. 2:14).

'Reconcile' is the verb of peace, the action of peace, and we see that reconciliation is why Christ came. He came, for one thing, to reconcile me and you to our Maker. Sin makes us God's enemies. We are traitors, and without the reconciliation of Christ our every thought and breath and movement is against God. What do traitors deserve? They deserve the death penalty. And not just any death penalty, because it is not just any treason. It is cosmic treason, in the famous words of R. C. Sproul, and therefore it deserves an eternal death. This recognition should create fear in the hearts of all people. But for the Christian, that terrifying judgment is precisely what Christ took for us on the cross: 'He descended into hell.' The full, everlasting curse was poured out on him in those moments of darkness and death. He dies as a substitute. He dies in our place. That is why Romans 5 wonderfully declares, 'Therefore, since we have been justified by faith, we have peace with God through our Lord Jesus Christ … For … while we were enemies we were reconciled to God by the death of his Son' (verses 1, 10).

Christ not only brings about a reconciliation between God and man, but also between God and creation. Colossians picks up where Romans leaves off and says that Jesus reconciled 'to himself all things, whether on earth or in heaven, making peace by the blood of his cross' (1:20). He has reconciled *all things*. Sin does not discriminate. When it entered our world, it polluted all of it. Decay, disease, and death riddle the entire globe. No rock, river, or flower is able to render back to God the complete perfection for which it was created. This whole world lacks peace, lacks that *shalom* and prosperity with which and for which God made it. But through his death Christ has guaranteed the eradication of this terrible blight we call sin, and has ensured that all things will be made new again. All things will be restored, so Paul says, 'For the creation was subjected to futility, not willingly, but because of him who subjected it, in hope that the creation itself will be set free from its bondage to corruption and obtain the freedom of the glory of the children of God' (Rom. 8:20, 21).

We do a disservice to the biblical conception of peace if we do not first recognize it as God's great purpose in redemption.

Internal Peace

Flowing from this eternal peace with God comes an internal peace in our souls, as well as an external peace with our neighbours. George Bethune defined the internal peace as 'that sweet composure, tranquil contentment' that is missing the 'easy fever which belongs to earthly passion.'[1] In New Testament language, peace and passions are opposites of one another. Passions are the fits and tantrums of a sinful heart, whereas peace is the calm of a heart that is trusting in God. Bethune ties these first three fruits of the Spirit together when he writes, 'The love is too secure in its satisfaction to be agitated, and the joy too deep and abiding for fitful transports.'[2] Peace is the heart at rest in God.

This peace is the kind that Jesus preached about when he said, 'do not be anxious about your life' (Matt. 6:25). As Jesus goes on to show in this great portion of the Sermon on the Mount, the reason we are not to worry about anything—about food, drink, or clothing—is because we have God as our heavenly Father: 'your heavenly Father knows that you need them all' (verse 32).

Do you see the connection between the eternal and internal peace? Do you see why we must first be right with God before our hearts can be at rest? If God is not my Father, then I have every reason to worry and be afraid. What confidence do I have that he will give 'good gifts' to me (Matt. 7:11)? It is my standing before God, my relationship with him, his adoption of me, that defines my peace—and the redemption wrought by Christ secures my standing and brings me into a right

---

[1] Bethune, *The Fruits of the Spirit*, p. 91.
[2] Bethune, *The Fruits of the Spirit*, p. 91.

relationship with Almighty God. The work of Christ is meant to expel anxiety and in its place produce peace. God has fully accepted us in the Beloved. To doubt such a reality is to be 'an enemy to your own peace,' in the words of the Puritan preacher John Flavel.[3] So I must first be forgiven, I must first be justified, I must first be adopted into his family and know that my forever is secure, before I can feel safe about my today. When you have that kind of certainty from God the Father, you will have peace, too.

All preachers know the stinging conviction of the aphorism, 'Practise what you preach.' But Jesus himself always put into perfect practice everything he preached, including his command to live without worry. The prime example has to be the scene on the Sea of Galilee in Mark 4:

> And a great windstorm arose, and the waves were breaking into the boat, so that the boat was already filling. But he was in the stern, asleep on the cushion. And they woke him and said to him, 'Teacher, do you not care that we are perishing?' And he awoke and rebuked the wind and said to the sea, 'Peace! Be still!' And the wind ceased, and there was a great calm. He said to them, 'Why are you so afraid? Have you still no faith?' And they were filled with great fear and said to one another, 'Who then is this, that even the wind and the sea obey him?'—Mark 4:37-41

[3] Quoted in Dane Ortlund, *Gentle and Lowly* (Wheaton, IL: Crossway, 2020), p. 187.

We see the calm of Jesus in this scene in that he is sleeping in the bottom of the boat while everyone on deck is fighting for their lives. Jesus could sleep because the storm was his, after all. As fully divine, he is the 'ruler of all nature.'[4] This is why he can command the wind and the waters. They were exemplifying that chaos from Genesis 1 to which God brought his *shalom*, and so Jesus fittingly commands them, 'Peace! Be still!' And they obey. He tells them to reflect his peaceful character. The creation will be like the Creator.

But as our mediator, as fully human, he trusted in his Father's protection. He was certain that he had a right relationship with God, not because he had been justified but because he was the justifier, and therefore no harm could befall him. He rested in the knowledge that his Father's will would be done, and a strong east wind and some rain could not thwart the plan of redemptive history. That trust that marked the character of Christ was lacking in his disciples. They panicked because they doubted the protection, provision, and good purpose of God. Again we see how faith in God is inextricably linked to our inner peace. When Jesus says, 'Have you still no faith?' He is saying, 'Do you still have no peace? Do you really doubt my Father's love for you? Do you think I would lead you into danger without bringing you through to safety?'

What is your response when the storms of life rock your boat? How do you react when your perfect little

---

[4] Unknown, 'Fairest Lord Jesus,' 1677.

kingdom gets toppled over by some unforeseen calamity such as debt, disease, death? Lockdowns, pandemics, protests, civil unrest? It really doesn't even take something that critical to throw us off course and open the floodgates of anxiety. A weird look from a co-worker, the need to write a strongly worded email, receiving a passive-aggressive text from someone in the family, traffic on the highway, not being able to pick out the right outfit in the morning—the things that can disrupt our peace are oftentimes pathetically petty. Oh, that we would repent of the lack of peace we often exhibit, even though we know we are united to the peace-producing Vine!

There is no getting around it, though. We will have turmoil in this world. Jesus acknowledges as much himself. Integral to the Christian faith is opening our hearts to the gift of peace that Christ has given us, so that we would rise above the tribulation in divinely-marked tranquillity. 'I have said these things to you, that in me you may have peace. In the world you will have tribulation. But take heart; I have overcome the world' (John 16:33; cf. Col. 3:15).

What a Saviour! And what a picture of this Saviour we are given in Mark 4! See him resting amidst the racket, and nestle yourself right there with him. Give him all your cares, worries, and fears. Give your trouble to him and you will discover Christ to be your calm in the storm. Give a world of worry to the One who has overcome the world.

As we grow in our union and communion with Christ, our inner peace will grow as well. This will come more easily to some of us than to others. Some are prone to anxiety and worry because of biological makeup, personal and family history, or other factors. But the Spirit can change all of that. Peter—hot-tempered, passionate Peter, who was panicking on deck during that storm with the other disciples—would come to take Jesus' words to heart, and cherish the gift of peace that he had been given. Later in his ministry he imitated his Saviour, sleeping peacefully in his cell moments before his expected execution at the hands of a cruel and unjust world—not even stirring up at the sudden appearance of an angel, who had to slap him awake (Acts 12)!

The thing to remember about this inner peace is its connection to our peace with God. The more we commune with God through worship, prayer, and Bible reading, and the more we enjoy the eternal peace that Christ secured on the cross, the more peaceful we will be in life. '[Peace] is an act of will,' says Christopher Wright, 'in which we *choose* not to worry, but to pray and trust God. And the whole Bible assures us that God can be trusted.'[5] In one of the most well-known passages on worry and anxiety, Paul connects the ideas of peace and prayer for us: 'do not be anxious about anything, but in everything by prayer and supplication with thanksgiving

---

[5] Christopher Wright, *Cultivating the Fruit of the Spirit* (Downers Grove, IL: InterVarsity Press, 2017), p. 59.

let your requests be made known to God. And the peace of God, which surpasses all understanding, will guard your hearts and your minds in Christ Jesus' (Phil. 4:6, 7).

It would not be a bad idea to consider how regularly we prevent our anxieties through the power of prayer. Oftentimes when we are stressed or anxious prayer is the last thing on our minds. But that is a mindset that requires repentance. We cannot have peace if we do not have prayer. Perhaps start now: confess your sin of neglecting God in prayer, and ask that he would make this fruit blossom in your life through a deeper commitment to Spirit-dependent prayer.

External Peace

As we have said, the logic of peace is as follows: it flows from God into our hearts, and from our hearts into our actions. We are to 'strive for peace with everyone' (Heb. 12:14), and to 'pursue what makes for peace and for mutual upbuilding' (Rom. 14:19). We do not content ourselves with peace as 'the brief glorious moment in history when everybody stands around reloading,' in the words of one cynic. The church—that is, those who have been justified by faith and therefore have peace with God—are supposed to have peace with one another. We are members of one body that is 'called to peace' (Col. 3:15, NIV). Paul writes in Ephesians 4:3 that we should be 'eager to maintain the unity of the Spirit in the bond of peace.' But the church is to lead the pursuit of peace in this world. John Owen said that 'there is no other Christian duty urged with more earnestness or vehemence than that of unity.'[6]

Why is peace-making so hard for us? For one reason, our sinful and selfish hearts cannot fathom any dignity to laying aside our preferences and even our rights. Yet this is the gospel way. Although at times every fibre of our being seems to scream the opposite, the truth of the Bible tells us that 'the anger of man does not produce the righteousness of God' (James 1:20). I think the other reason we struggle with maintaining peace is that we often have a misconception of it. We think that peace-making means either (a) passivity or (b) compromising our values. It means neither.

Peace-making is certainly not passive: we are told to 'pursue' it (Psa. 34:14; cf. Rom. 14:19; 2 Tim. 2:22; 1 Pet. 3:11)—the Hebrew word conveys the idea of chasing after something intensely with the intention of overtaking it. As the great Dutch thinker of the second Reformation, Wilhelmus à Brakel, reminds us, if we want to be at peace with one another, 'a peacemaker [has to be] continually at war with the devil, the world, and his corrupt flesh—with them he neither desires nor seeks to be at peace. The more he hates and opposes them, the better he likes it.'[7] Similarly, Owen puts it in visceral language when he

---

[6] John Owen, *Duties of Christian Fellowship: A Manual for Church Members* (Edinburgh: Banner of Truth Trust, 2020), p. 44.
[7] Wilhelmus à Brakel, *The Christian's Reasonable Service*, 4:92.

writes that we are 'daily to strike at the root of all division.'[8] So do not think that maintaining unity with your neighbours is a call you can fulfil by sitting back on your couch, never even engaging your neighbour. That is to indulge the sinful desires of the flesh. We need to crucify that in order to engage the world, and in such a way that we are prepared to pay great costs to attain peace. 2 Corinthians 13:11 says, 'Agree with one another, live in peace'—the 'one another' implies community, the 'live' implies activity. Peace is neither private nor passive.

Nor is it compromise. When we sacrifice truth and godliness at that altar of peace, we have actually sacrificed peace along with them. The Spirit that is producing peace in our hearts is called by Christ three times the 'Spirit of truth' (John 14:17; 15:26; 16:13). He will not call us to one virtue at the expense of another.

This is quite a charge upon Christians of our day and age, as people are seemingly more and more offended at encountering ideas that are not consistent with their worldview. This is the age of the so-called 'snowflake' generation, which cannot bear the thought of being told they are wrong. This has spread through our culture, creating a hypersensitivity to the potential for offending someone. But the Bible never says that causing offence is necessarily a sin. Jesus himself is the 'rock of offence' (Rom. 9:33), and our gospel proclamation will cause people to stumble. That's okay. That is why the

[8] Owen, *Duties of Christian Fellowship*, p. 46.

biblical command is not 'at all times, in every situation whatsoever, no matter what, live peaceably with all.' No, instead it is, *'If possible*, so far as it depends on you, live peaceably with all' (Rom. 12:18, emphasis added).

This is no easy task, and there are more opportunities than we would care to admit where we could be enacting peace. Yet our motivation comes from that sweet benediction of Jesus: 'Blessed are the peacemakers' (Matt. 5:9). Again, these are not words that Jesus merely spoke, but words that he embodied in practice and principle. Perhaps the most powerful example is on the Mount of Olives, at his betrayal. We read in Luke 22:47-51,

> While he was still speaking, there came a crowd, and the man called Judas, one of the twelve, was leading them. He drew near to Jesus to kiss him, but Jesus said to him, 'Judas, would you betray the Son of Man with a kiss?' And when those who were around him saw what would follow, they said, 'Lord, shall we strike with the sword?' And one of them struck the servant of the high priest and cut off his right ear. But Jesus said, 'No more of this!' And he touched his ear and healed him.

See peace-making in action here. Unlike the disciples, Jesus does not respond in defence. Peace is not at the cost of truth or godliness, but it can be at the cost of our own comfort, reputation, perhaps even safety. The hand of peace never reaches for the weapons of this world, whether they be physical clubs or Facebook comments.

The hand of peace reaches to restore: reaching out to heal those who are wounded, even if they deserved it. Peace-making knows nothing of revenge—something that never belongs to us (Deut. 32:35), no matter what wrongs are done to us.

And of course, as we have already considered, peace-making is reconciliatory. The point is to bring back together divided groups. And so in this scene Jesus will go with his accusers, endure their mock trial, and be killed on a cross. It was my sin, it was your sin, that led him to the cross. Yet, in the wonderful twist of God's gospel, it is that very cross where he secures our peace (Col. 1:20).

There are two beams to a cross: the vertical beam, reminding us of the peace between us and our Maker, as well as the horizontal beam, peace between us and our neighbour. And so, as his hands are stretched out across that beam, see him reaching towards us in peace, so that we would have every reason to reach out to the world in the same way. When we do so, we join in the greatest of all God's works: peace-making.

4

CONSIDER HIM WHO ENDURED

I F you have heard it once, you have heard it a thousand
times. 'Patience is a virtue.' I imagine the majority of
people who have quipped this line haven't realized just how
right they are. A virtue indeed! It is nestled right here at
the start of what some scholars consider to be the second
of three triads in the fruit of the Spirit, these three focusing
on 'social virtues': patience, kindness, and goodness.[1]

What comes to mind when you consider patience?
Many think about the ability to stand in line at an
amusement park for hours and hours, with the cruel,
hot sun beating down upon us, children tugging at our
pockets and whining about their boredom, without
losing our minds. Or the ability to be stuck in traffic
on the commute to work and refrain from engaging in
any driver-to-driver off-colour communication. Perhaps
patience is recognizing life goes on even if the Amazon

[1] See Stott, *Galatians*, p. 147.

Prime package hasn't arrived on time. Or maybe we think true patience is measured by how long we can wait on the tarmac without murmuring a complaint to the passenger next to us.

It is certainly true that the ability to have a calm disposition even through long stretches of discomfort or personal inconvenience is a good thing, and a godly thing—and I know I lack it! In this sense, my impatience is most clearly manifested in home projects. I love the concept of completing them, in my mind I have a vision of what they should and will (I hope!) look like, and I just want to get started. I rarely wait to see if I have the right tools. I do not sleep on a thought and see if I still like it in the morning. I do not adhere to the wisdom of 'measure twice, cut once,' and all of these things come back to bite me. Things always end up taking me longer than they should and I inevitably lose my temper. My anger is born out of the impatience with which I head into the project. Impatience and anger go hand in hand.

So is this what Paul is talking about here? Is he talking about our ability to keep our cool in a long line, whether at an amusement park or on the highway? Is the fruit of the Spirit the wisdom to calmly and clearly think through projects before you dive into them? That is undoubtedly an aspect of it. However, I think any of this is far too weak a conception of what the Bible is teaching. Patience *is* a virtue, but likely not in the way you are thinking of when you hear that aphorism.

To help us better understand what the Spirit is producing in the new hearts of redeemed and restored Christians, there are two other words we should consider instead of patience: *forbearance* and *long-suffering*. These are a little bit more archaic but they are also a lot more accurate. And while closely related, they each highlight a different aspect of this spiritual fruit of patience. As an umbrella term, *patience* is still helpful. J. I. Packer defines it as 'the Christlike reaction to all that is maddening.'[2] But let us focus our study on these alternative terms:

> *Forbearance* is the loving tolerance shown towards the weaknesses, failures, and sins of others against us, responding in compassion and mercy and not retaliating in judgment or vengeance, no matter how warranted that may be.
>
> *Long-suffering* is the ability to endure trials and hardships with joy, without losing faith in God or his good purposes.

Forbearance

First up is forbearance. We are on fairly solid ground to conclude that this is the type of patience that Paul wants to highlight in Galatians 5 when we compare his use of the word elsewhere. In 1 Thessalonians 5:14 he writes, 'And we urge you, brothers, admonish the idle, encourage the fainthearted, help the weak.' Here he has listed

---

[2] J. I. Packer, *Knowing and Doing the Will of God* (Ann Arbor, MI: Servant, 1995), p. 293.

three groups of people that need particular attention in ministry. John Stott says they could be considered 'the problem children of the church.'[3] They each have personality traits that will not change overnight. You can imagine the frustration of trying to instil a work ethic in someone who is prone to laziness, for example. But Paul concludes the verse with one more exhortation: 'be patient with them all.' In response to the weaknesses of others, we are to display loving tolerance. This virtue is essential for the church as she faces issues that tend to polarize and divide her members. It is so easy to look at fellow Christians and think, 'Why don't they just *get* it? Why don't they just see things like I do?' The difficulty or disappointment of others does not validate our dismissal of them; rather it necessitates our forbearance with them.

In response to the weaknesses of others, we are to display loving tolerance. The same is true in response to the sins of others, as Colossians 3:12, 13 tells us. Interestingly, in verse 12 Paul gives a list that looks a lot like the fruit of the Spirit, which he concludes with patience. But then in verse 13 he goes on to give us a further explanation of what that patience really means: 'Put on then, as God's chosen ones, holy and beloved, compassionate hearts, kindness, humility, meekness, and patience, *bearing with one another and, if one has a complaint against another,*

[3] John Stott, *The Message of 1 & 2 Thessalonians* (Downers Grove, IL: InterVarsity Press, 1994), p. 122.

forgiving each other; as the Lord has forgiven you, so you also must forgive' (emphasis added).

What Paul says here is so important. He says that the very forgiveness that we have received—our eternity in heaven—is based upon the patient forbearance of God in Christ Jesus. James Montgomery Boice writes that 'God is the supreme example of patience in his dealings with rebellious people.'[4] All of history is proof of this. The moment Adam and Eve sinned could have been the end. Judgment might justly have come at that very moment. And while the pronouncement of judgment did come immediately after the sin, Adam and Eve did not immediately die the death that was deserved for eating the forbidden fruit. They lived long under the forbearance of God so that they might learn of his love and mercy.

Patience is who God is. The pinnacle of God's revelation in the Old Testament comes in Exodus 34 when he allows his glory to pass by Moses on Mount Sinai. And when that happens, God declares a definition for himself: 'The LORD, the LORD, a God merciful and gracious, slow to anger, and abounding in steadfast love and faithfulness.' *Slow to anger* captures perfectly the idea of patience that we are after here, and it captures perfectly the character of God. It is a phrase that will go on to be heralded again and again in praise by Old Testament writers (e.g., Num. 14:18; Psa. 103:8; 145:8; Joel 2:13). As one theologian explains:

[4] James Montgomery Boice, *Foundations of the Christian Faith* (Downers Grove, IL: InterVarsity, 1986), p. 385.

> *Slow to anger* does not present the Lord as a frustrated deity who eventually loses patience and strikes out against those who have thwarted him. It rather acknowledges that the Lord is reluctant to act against his creation, even when it is in rebellion against him. He waits long to give the sinner opportunity to return in repentance.[5]

In Jesus Christ, God's 'slow to anger' goes from declaration to actual flesh-and-bone incarnation. Just as with the other fruits of the Spirit, Jesus is the embodiment of patience. His life and ministry is marked by forbearance towards sinners. He is the ultimate Judge (John 5:22), and yet he comes and lays the gavel aside to instead embrace those who would repent in love and mercy.

We are often so zealous for swift justice and retribution, but Jesus shows us a better way. When he is rejected by a village of Samaritans, his disciples are indignant and ask, '"Lord, do you want us to tell fire to come down from heaven and consume them?" But he turned and rebuked them' (Luke 9:54, 55). A hasty response of damnation would be entirely inconsistent with Jesus' patient and compassionate heart—his heart which desires to save and restore wayward sinners, not condemn them. And so he rebukes his disciples, 'For the Son of man is not come to destroy men's lives, but to save them' (verse 56, KJV).

---

[5] John L. Mackay, *Exodus* (Fearn, Ross-shire: Christian Focus, 2001), p. 563.

Where would we be if every sin received hellfire and brimstone? We would be utterly lost! Thanks be to God for the patience of Jesus! Thanks be to God for the sterling character of Christ! Paul recognized that: Paul, who prior to his conversion was Saul of Tarsus, persecutor *par excellence* of Christ and his church. He attributes his salvation to the kind, tolerant forbearance of Christ: 'But I received mercy for this reason, that in me, as the foremost [sinner], Jesus Christ might display his *perfect patience* as an example to those who were to believe in him for eternal life' (1 Tim. 1:16, emphasis added). Praise God for his perfect patience!

Repent

The forbearance of Christ should elicit two responses from us. The first is *repentance*. That is the main point that Paul is making in the aforementioned verse. 'Take me as an example,' he is saying. 'If Christ can be patient with even one such as me and bring me to salvation, he can do the same for you!' If we think our sins are so great as to prevent us coming to God and that we have missed our chance at receiving his mercy, what we have really missed is an understanding of the patience of Christ. As Paul exemplifies, the greater the sin and the sinner, the greater the experience of the forbearance of God in the gospel. So Thomas Goodwin can write, in his classic book *The Heart of Christ*,

> There is comfort concerning such infirmities, in that your very sins move him to pity more than to anger ...

> the greater the misery is, the more is the pity when the party is beloved. Now of all miseries, sin is the greatest … And [Christ], loving your persons, and hating only the sin, his hatred shall all fall, and that only upon the sin, to free you of it by its ruin and destruction, but his affections shall be the more drawn out to you … Therefore, fear not.[6]

Indeed, fear not! Turn to God in repentance and receive his forbearing love! Recognize that God 'is *patient* toward you, not wishing that any should perish, but that all should reach repentance' (2 Pet. 3:9, emphasis added). Recognize that 'now is the favourable time; behold, now is the day of salvation' (2 Cor. 6:2).

But do not waste God's patience. It will not be forever. God is *slow* to anger, but that does not mean he will never become angry. 'The wrath of God is coming' (Col. 3:6). Tomorrow is not guaranteed to you. In the words of the Puritan Thomas Watson, 'Many are now in hell that purposed to repent.' In addition to this chilling warning of procrastinators now languishing in eternal gloomy darkness, Watson also offers a simple and logical exhortation: 'The sooner you repent, the fewer sins you will have to answer for.'[7] Put all these together, and what reason do you have *not* to repent?

---

[6] Thomas Goodwin, *The Heart of Christ in Heaven towards Sinners on Earth* (Edinburgh: Banner of Truth Trust, 2021), pp. 115-116.

[7] Thomas Watson, *The Doctrine of Repentance* (Edinburgh: Banner of Truth Trust, 1994), pp. 86-87.

In all sobriety and contrition, know full well that Christ will come again, and when he does he will come as judge. So see now how he bears with all of your weaknesses, failures, and sins, and run to his loving embrace before it's too late. Plead for the grace of repentance and the forgiveness of sins—right now.

Represent

Once we have repented and turned to Christ for salvation, which is the proper first response to his forbearance, then we are in a position to enact the second response, which is to *represent* Christ by showing this same patience to those who sin against us. This is the very point of Paul's teaching in Colossians, is it not? 'Bearing with one another and, if one has a complaint against another, forgiving each other; *as the Lord has forgiven you, so you also must forgive*' (3:13, emphasis added). The forbearance we have received from Christ is to then flow from us to those around us. It is certainly one thing to love those whom we find easy company, to enjoy those who do not irk us. But that is not all love is. Love is *patient*, according to 1 Corinthians 13, and Jesus himself says, 'For if you love those who love you, what reward do you have?' (Matt. 5:46).

Peter, as he often does, asks the question that is on all of our minds: *how long* do I have to keep putting up with my brother's sins against me? Seven times?! (Matt. 18:21.) This is a question about patience. And what a foolish question it is, in light of the gospel mercy that we have received. We want to quantify what is expected of us in terms of our forbearance of others, when the gospel is about the limitless love of God poured out upon us despite our infinite, immeasurable, and unquantifiable sin! Having the Spirit of Christ opens our eyes to that reality, as well as opening our hearts to consistently forgive and forbear those who do us wrong.

Long-suffering

When considering the biblical conception of patience, a term closely related to forbearance is long-suffering. Long-suffering is the ability to endure hardships and tri-als, whether they be at the hands of other sinners or not. Long-suffering, in Old Testament terms, is that blessed quality of waiting on the Lord—'I waited patiently for the LORD; he inclined to me and heard my cry' (Psa. 40:1). Since every trial comes from the hand of God, our ability to endure the maddening aspects of life is proportionate to our understanding of the providence of God. Spiritual patience depends upon a love and trust in the providence of God. Hence à Brakel defines this fruit as 'the believer's spiritual strength which he has in God whereby he, in the performance of his duty, will-ingly, with composure, joyfully, and steadfastly endures all the vicissitudes of life, *having a hope that the outcome will be well.*'[8]

---

[8] à Brakel, *The Christian's Reasonable Service*, 3:413, emphasis added.

How can we have such a hope? Because we know that God is working all things for our eternal good. We cannot attain heaven unless we go through the trials of earth (Acts 14:22). And so it is the hope of glory that fuels the long-suffering needed to get through the ups and downs of this life. 'When there is no longer hope,' à Brakel writes, 'patience will no longer be exercised. There is no patience in hell due to the absence of hope.'[9] But for now we have an abundance of hope. The best is yet to come! And so Paul tells us that 'if we hope for what we do not see, we wait for it with patience' (Rom. 8:25).

The word for 'patience' in Romans 8 is not the same Greek word that we have seen thus far in this study. It is a word that is elsewhere translated 'endurance,' connoting the idea of cheerful constancy no matter the circumstances. This is certainly a fruit of the Spirit of Christ, for as we look to his life we see a consistent display of long-suffering and endurance despite profound hardships. He patiently endured temptation (Matt. 4). He patiently endured the difficulty of not-knowing: 'But concerning that day or that hour, no one knows, not even the angels in heaven, nor the Son, but only the Father' (Mark 13:32). He was able to entrust himself and his future to the Father that he knew loved him well and was executing a perfect plan. He endured profound mistreatment (Isa. 53:7). The author of the letter to the Hebrews wants us to look to Christ as our pioneer in the way of long-suffering: '*Consider him*

[9] à Brakel, *The Christian's Reasonable Service*, 3:417.

who endured from sinners such hostility against himself, so that you may not grow weary or fainthearted' (Heb. 12:3, emphasis added). As we are prone to feel fed up with the waiting we are called to in this life, we remember all that Christ endured for us. The burdens we are called to shoulder will always pale in comparison to his.

The most important thing to grasp, though, is not that Jesus is our example of endurance during the tribulation; he *is* our endurance during the tribulation. The Apostle John, writing from a position of great persecution on the Island of Patmos, describes himself to the church as 'your brother and partner in the tribulation and the kingdom and the patient endurance *that are in Jesus*' (Rev. 1:9, emphasis added). The endurance we need for the tribulations that will lead to the kingdom is found in Christ.

Do you exhibit this important virtue in your life? Are you convicted that you are not bearing fruit in this respect, to the glory of God? Do you want to grow in patience and endurance? Then you must grow in your union and communion with the Saviour. It is then you come to realize that the only thing that keeps you steady is the fact that he will never let you go. The Christian is ultimately not crushed under the perplexity and distress of the maddening troubles of this world because Christ has persevered for us, and when we have his Spirit we have his perseverance, too. He is keeping you, dear Christian. We have a cross to patiently bear in this life, yes, but we remember the words of Samuel Rutherford:

'The weightiest end of the cross of Christ that is laid upon you lieth upon your strong Saviour.'[10]

With this we should understand that *only good things* can come from our long-suffering through the trials of this life and faithful waiting upon God. It is sometimes difficult to see that from our vantage point, without having the big picture in view. Jean-Henri Fabri is a great illustration of this point. He was a renowned French naturalist, considered by some to be the greatest naturalist who ever lived. And yet he did not begin the main part of his work until he was sixty, and he was not discovered by fame until ninety. He completed all of his work without the proper scientific instruments or a laboratory. But he said his two greatest instruments were 'time' and 'patience.'[11]

Patience pays off for all, but for the Christian it pays off in eternal dividends. Our faithful patience leads us to eternal life in the presence of our forbearing, long-suffering God. So, with the psalmist, take hope. 'I believe that I shall look upon the goodness of the LORD in the land of the living! Wait for the LORD; be strong, and let your heart take courage; wait for the LORD!' (Psa. 27:13, 14).

---

[10] Samuel Rutherford, *Letters of Samuel Rutherford* (Edinburgh: Banner of Truth Trust, 2012), p. 34.

[11] Donald Grey Barnhouse, *Let Me Illustrate* (Grand Rapids, MI: Revell, 1967), p. 302.

5

WHEN KINDNESS APPEARED

KINDNESS is a concept that is so expansive, complex, and nuanced that it eludes a simple definition, and yet we know it when we experience it. One nineteenth-century American epigrammatist quipped that kindness is 'a language which the dumb can speak, and the deaf can understand.'[1]

Perhaps we can put a finer point on it by saying that kindness is a disposition of the heart that seeks the welfare of others. It is captured well in Paul's exhortation: 'Let each of you look not only to his own interests, but also to the interests of others' (Phil. 2:4). To fill out our definition a little more, we should add that this looking to the interest and wellbeing of others is independent of their deserving it or not, and also independent of any services in return. Kindness is to do good to others for the sake of doing good to others.

[1] Christian Nestell Bovee, *Thoughts, Feelings and Fancies* (New York: Wiley & Halsted, 1857), p. 109.

Actually, far from freeing us from the obligation to be kind, it would be right to say that someone's *not* deserving kindness prompts us all the more to show it. 'As an expression of the gospel, it does not treat people as they deserve, but on the basis of compassionate care.'[2] When we look at some of the New Testament instructions for being kind, we find that they come precisely in the context of when it is most difficult and least natural to do so. Perhaps this is why kindness follows on the heels of patience, just as it does in 1 Corinthians 13 ('love is patient and kind,' verse 4). One of the ways we best love others is by showing them kindness through our forbearance and long-suffering with their faults.

Ephesians 4:32 correlates kindness and forgiveness: 'Be kind to one another, tenderhearted, forgiving one another, as God in Christ forgave you.' Jesus says, 'But love your enemies, and do good, and lend, expecting nothing in return, and your reward will be great, and you will be sons of the Most High, *for he is kind to the ungrateful and the evil*. Be merciful, even as your Father is merciful' (Luke 6:35, 36, emphasis added). We are to be merciful to people who have wronged us, to love those who hate us, and to do it all expecting nothing in return. Why? Because then we prove ourselves children of God himself, who is kind even to the wicked.

Indeed, one of the Old Testament's favourite ways to describe the heart and character of God is to say that he

---

[2] Stanley D. Gale, *A Vine-Ripened Life* (Grand Rapids, MI: Reformation Heritage Books, 2014), p. 84.

is kind. The Old Testament authors ascribe this attribute to God with the rich Hebrew word *hesed*. The word is so deep in meaning that it is translated many different ways when brought into English. Sometimes it is rendered *love*, or *faithfulness*, or *mercy*. In the classic King James Version it is most often rendered as 'lovingkindness.' And so we have these beautiful expressions of the psalmists and the prophets extolling God because he is kind:

> 'How excellent is thy lovingkindness, O God! therefore the children of men put their trust under the shadow of thy wings.' (Psa. 36:7, KJV)

> 'Because thy lovingkindness is better than life, my lips shall praise thee.' (Psa. 63:3, KJV)

> 'Cause me to hear thy lovingkindness in the morning; for in thee do I trust: cause me to know the way wherein I should walk; for I lift up my soul unto thee.' (Psa. 143:8, KJV)

> 'The LORD is righteous in all his ways and kind in all his works.' (Psa. 145:17, ESV)

> 'I will tell of the kindnesses of the LORD, the deeds for which he is to be praised, according to all the LORD has done for us—yes, the many good things he has done for Israel, according to his compassion and many kindnesses.' (Isa. 63:7, NIV)

> '"But let the one who boasts boast about this: that they have the understanding to know me, that I am the

LORD, who exercises kindness, justice and righteousness on earth, for in these I delight," declares the LORD.' (Jer. 9:24, NIV)

What a God is our God! From these passages we learn that kindness is a key component of the character of God. You cannot know who God is without knowing that he is kind. There is no conception of God apart from kindness. In his very heart, in the core of his being, he is concerned with the welfare of others. He desires to see others flourish and succeed. He is kind; he is kindness.

Kindness Incarnate

With this in mind, Paul's statement in <u>Titus 3:4, 5</u> makes perfect sense: 'But when the kindness and love of God our Saviour appeared, he saved us, not because of righteous things we had done, but because of his mercy' (NIV). This is incarnation language. Paul is speaking about the revelation of God in human form. John would say 'the Word became flesh' (1:14); Paul says, 'the kindness and love of God our Saviour appeared.'

Think about that for a moment. When speaking of the most stupendous moment in all of human history—when heaven comes down to earth, when God steps into his own creation and becomes man, when the plan of redemption enters its most decisive phase—Paul can simply say that 'kindness appeared.' Maybe we too often think that kindness is inconsequential, as though it were nothing more than holding the door for someone, or flashing a smile to a passer-by. Yet according to the biblical texts we have seen, kindness is no small thing. It is God come to earth, and it is our souls sent to heaven. 'When the kindness of God appeared, he *saved us* …'

If we believe the incarnation is the physical, tangible manifestation of all that is in God, then it must be the physical, tangible manifestation of kindness as well. Up until this point the kindness of God was only ever known or experienced insofar as it was mediated through God's providence. But now there is no mediation. Two thousand years ago, in Bethlehem, outside an overcrowded inn during a Roman census, the people of God were brought face-to-face with kindness itself. This is how God most abundantly shows his concern for the welfare and wellbeing of others. This is how he is faithful to his covenant promises and generous in his mercy and love. It is all seen there in the face of that baby boy. When Mary wrapped her child in swaddling clothes, she was also wrapping up Kindness. Kindness was in her very arms.

Three Scenes

As Jesus grows and enters into his long-foretold public ministry, we begin to see more clearly how he is kindness incarnate. He never once did anything out of selfish ambition. He never manipulated others. He was always seeking their welfare. Consider three examples that bring this to the fore for us.

Kindly feeding

The first is Mark 6:30-44 and the famous scene where Jesus feeds the five thousand. The episode begins with Jesus seeking rest: he withdraws to a quiet spot to be alone and to recuperate from his exhausting ministry. And yet the people follow him. They are desperate for him, in fact. What is the response from Jesus? Maybe we should consider first how *we* respond to the 'inconvenient' needs and demands of others. What is your response when someone knocks on the door just as you are getting ready for a long-awaited nap? What is your response when your kids creep into the living room after you already have read stories, tucked in, sung lullabies, found the stuffed animals, re-tucked, given kisses, and were finally about to have that much-deserved glass of wine? You get the picture! 'Kindness' is likely not the immediate reaction many of us have. If we are being honest, we recognize that our schedules, our wants, our preferences are often top priority, and the welfare of others is a distant second.

Yet what does Jesus do here? The text says that he 'had compassion' on the crowds (verse 34). He did not turn them away, but was instead 'inwardly moved so as to have to do something about it.'[3] In other words, he was moved to kindness. And this kindness takes on at least two aspects.

[3] Donald English, *The Message of Mark* (Downers Grove, IL: InterVarsity Press, 1992), p. 134.

First, he teaches them. He gears up for yet another exhausting evening of ministry and he preaches the gospel of the kingdom. Jesus understood that the people's spiritual need to hear the Good News was greater and more important than his need for rest.

Second, he recognizes their need for food, a very serious need, and he meets it. Remember, the scene takes place out in the middle of nowhere (a 'desolate' place, verse 35). There were no gas stations nearby to run into and grab some snacks. Whereas the disciples pragmatically think, 'We need to wrap this thing up so the people can head home and eat,' Jesus recognizes that to force the people to do so would make them choose between their bellies and being with the Messiah. Rather, he feeds them—'and they all ate and were satisfied' (verse 42). He shows them that the One who meets their *spiritual* need is the One who will meet their *every* need. He has an inward compassion for them, and his compassion pours forth in acts of kindness. It is the most famous miracle in the Bible, the only one recorded in all four Gospels, and it is a miracle of kindness.

Kindly healing

A second example is Jesus' encounter with the leper at the start of Matthew 8. There are many accounts of Jesus healing people who are sick and diseased. The particular import of this story is that leprosy was a condition that made one ceremonially unclean. Anyone who had leprosy and anyone who came into contact with a leper was unfit for coming into the pure place of worship. For the people of Jesus' day that access to the temple was everything: your status as a worshipper defined your status as a human being. You can begin to understand how spiritually disastrous the diagnosis of leprosy was! Leprosy was a socially shameful disease as well, as those who contracted it had to go about the town shouting 'Unclean! Unclean!' to make sure other people knew to stay clear away. To be unclean, to be apart from the temple, signified that one was cursed by God. It did not get much worse than leprosy in the ancient world.[4]

But this leper in Matthew 8 knows in his heart that Jesus can change all of that: 'Lord, if you will, you can make me clean' (verse 2). Note two astounding things about Jesus' response. First, he touches the man: 'And Jesus stretched out his hand and touched him' (verse 3). Anyone else would have recoiled in fear and disgust, turned, and run. Why be barred from the presence of God yourself on account of someone who was going to die anyway? But Jesus touches this poor individual. Kindness always turns towards those in need, never away. No contact would compromise his holiness and purity—quite the opposite. To come into contact with the living God is to be consumed with his holiness. Here we have a picture of the curative, sanctifying power of the gospel. The Jewish system at best could only protect

---

[4] See Leviticus 13:45, 46.

other worshipers from contracting leprosy. But Jesus Christ—love, compassion, and kindness incarnate—can actually heal the leper.

The second thing to note about Jesus' response, beyond his gracious touch, is his verbal response. The man says to Jesus, 'Lord, if you *will*.' In other words, 'If you would be willing, if you want, if you desire, please heal me!' The leper recognizes that to receive this kindness from Christ, Jesus must first have a disposition to show it. And what does Jesus say? 'I will; be clean' (verse 3). He *wants* to help this man. Real Spirit-prompted kindness *desires* the welfare of others. We can do things that on the surface seem kind, but if they are motivated by a begrudging obligation on the inside, they are not produced by the Holy Spirit. Real kindness *wills*.

Kindly forgiving

One final look into the kindness of Christ comes from his dying words on the cross, as recorded in Luke 23:34. In response to the mob, to the injustice, to the hatred and the violence, Jesus prays, with belaboured gasps: 'Father, forgive them, for they know not what they do.' The pinnacle of the manifestation of God's kindness is found in the forgiveness he freely bestows even upon those who have sinned against him. Do you know that kindness? He is eager to show it to you.

I have listened to thousands upon thousands of sermons in my life, and have profited from the majority.

But I don't think I am alone in admitting that nearly all sermons I have heard have been long forgotten. *Nearly* all. One of the rare and precious ones that has stuck with me was when I was in my second year of undergraduate studies. I remember that feeling of being fixed under the power of God's preached word as though it only happened this morning. That day, our church welcomed a guest preacher, Dr Ligon Duncan, who addressed the kindness of Christ in forgiving sinners so powerfully it was almost as if I had never even considered it before! Let me share:

> All of us have sins that if our friends, even in this room, were to know we would be humiliated, mortally embarrassed. The great Scottish preacher Thomas Boston once said, 'If men knew my heart I would not have four friends left in Scotland.' And I want you to know that those sins about which you are most humiliated, about which you are most embarrassed, about which you greatly fear anyone knowing—if you trust in Christ, God has laid those sins on your Saviour. He has borne the due penalty for them. He has been cursed for those sins, humiliated and stricken down for those sins. He has borne what you deserve so that you may receive what he deserves. That's why Jesus is on the cross—so that you might be forgiven and accepted.[5]

[5] J. Ligon Duncan III, 'The Gospel Ministry of Reconciliation', sermon preached at Tenth Presbyterian Church, Philadelphia, PA on 22 April 2012.

The sin that would kill most friendships constitutes our friendship with Christ. He knows all that we have done, and he doesn't turn us away. In kindness, he draws us even closer to himself: 'Father, forgive them.' Remember, the spiritual fruit of kindness is intimately connected with the idea of mercy and forgiveness. The greatest kindness we can ever show is the kindness of forgiving and restoring someone who has done us wrong.

Just Be Kind?

So go and do that. Just be kind.

That is what some of the signs in my neighbourhood are telling me to do, anyway. As I write this, many American homes have colourful yard signs with the declaration 'In this house we believe …' followed by a list of tenets to what can only be described as a modern secular creed. Rounding out the whole list is this impressive statement: 'Kindness is everything.' In today's world, the transcendent imperative upon all moral creatures is to be kind to one another. That is quite a claim.

There's another grassroots social movement that declares that kindness is 'easy.' What started as an after-school club in 2015 has grown into a worldwide phenomenon. Kids in central Indiana are making and selling artwork that simply says 'Just Be Kind' and then donating the profits to charitable organizations. The slogan for the movement is equally punchy: 'It's easy.'[6] Is

[6] Justin N. Poythress, 'How Jesus Transforms "Just Be Kind"', The

it, though? According to these two secular movements, kindness is supposedly both everything *and* easy.

We have seen Jesus showing kindness by meeting physical needs, by risking social ridicule out of a sincere desire to help the poor, and by granting forgiveness to the ungrateful and evil. Is that easy? If it is, go and do it. But we all know something deep in our hearts: it's *not* so easy. In fact, the Bible tells us as much. In Romans 3:12 we are told that 'no one does good, not even one.' The word for 'good' is in fact the same word translated as 'kindness' elsewhere. Scripture's indictment on the human condition is that no one, not a single person, is naturally kind to others. The virtue that is supposedly 'everything' is in reality rejected by everyone. The act that is branded as 'easy' proves to be staggeringly difficult.

But that's okay—at least in the sense that the Bible does not tell us on the one hand that showing kindness is a natural impossibility, and then on the other hand command us to 'just be kind—it's easy.' Consider the examples we looked at of the kindness of Jesus. How do we situate ourselves in these various stories? What is the takeaway for you? What do those stories have to do with me and you? The *main* point is never, 'Now go be just like Jesus.' The point is to see how we ourselves have personally benefitted from the character of Christ. He has come to us and met our needs, reached out and

Gospel Coalition, 11 Nov. 2019, https://www.thegospelcoalition.org/article/jesus-transforms-just-kind/.

touched us when all others would recoil, has willed our happiness when the rest of the world was consumed with itself, has offered us forgiveness even though we have hated him and sinned against him in grievous ways.

The point is to see the ways in which Jesus shows kindness to *us*. That must be where we begin. And from there, we find the spiritual fuel necessary to show the same type of kindness to others. We can only give to others whatever we have first received from God. Phil Ryken says that '*knowing* the kindness of God enables us to start *showing* the kindness of God.'[7]

Or we could put it this way: before the spiritual fruit of kindness can appear in our hearts and lives, it first had to appear in Bethlehem. It first had to walk this earth, serve the world, live our life and die our death. Putting your faith in the appearance of God's kindness in the person of Jesus Christ will produce that very same virtue in your own heart.

Again, do not underestimate kindness. It is one of the most powerful tools we have to bear witness to Christ. In the ancient church, the theologian Tertullian records that Christians were often recognized by the pagan world for their acts of charity and kindness. The Greek word that we have been looking at in these various New Testament passages is *chrēstotēs*. A pun developed in the third century where Christians were called '*Chrēstiani*'

---

[7] Phil Ryken, *Loving the Way Jesus Loves* (Wheaton, IL: Crossway, 2012), p. 41.

instead of '*Christiani*'—the former being a play on that Greek word. Literally, Christians were called the 'kindness people.'[8] Fast-forward a hundred years and Augustine, perhaps the most influential theologian of all time, recounts in his *Confessions* that what endeared him to his mentor, Ambrose of Milan, was not simply his preaching or teaching, but that Ambrose showed kindness to him.[9]

Never underestimate the powerful effect that an act of kindness can have on someone. When we show kindness, we show Christ. We cannot save anyone from their sins by our kindness, but we can witness to the kindness that does save. Kindness is not everything, but Jesus is. And so a compassionate, charitable, kind act today can open up the way for someone else to know and experience God's everlasting kindness. For the promise of the gospel is that 'in the coming ages [God] might show the immeasurable riches of his grace in kindness toward us in Christ Jesus' (Eph. 2:7).

[8] Ryken, *Loving the Way Jesus Loves*, p. 43.
[9] St Augustine, *Confessions*, 5.13.23.

6

'WHY DO YOU CALL ME GOOD?'

ANCIENT philosophers often spoke of the concept of 'being' as comprising goodness, truth, and beauty. To them, this trilogy represents only the ideals of this world, but not this world itself. Thus they are sometimes referred to as the 'transcendentals'—virtues and concepts that transcend anything we could ever really experience in this life. So, for example, according to Plato, the Good cannot be found here; our world is a shadow of the Good. The Good is ultimate reality, even God—at least 'God' in the sense that Plato could not conceive of any being greater than the Good.

Several hundred years later, Jesus would almost seem to confirm this notion that goodness lies outside of our grasp, when he says to an anxious and earnest rich young ruler, 'Why do you call me good? No one is good except God alone' (Luke 18:19). This word used here is the root word we find in Galatians 5:22, 'The fruit of the Spirit is … *goodness*.' A self-help, pull-yourself-up-by-your-bootstraps approach to the fruit of the Spirit, which says that you just need to follow a few steps to evince and cultivate these virtues on your own, will be roundly aborted by a careful reflection on Jesus' words: 'No one is good except God.'

Indeed, goodness begins with God, and that is where we rightly begin in this study as well. à Brakel places goodness at 'the very essence of God's being.'[1] Spelling it out even more clearly, and with rhapsodic wonder, English theologian Stephen Charnock in his book on the attributes of God writes,

> This is the true and genuine character of God. He is good, he is goodness, good in himself, good in his essence, good in the highest degree, possessing whatsoever is comely, excellent, desirable; the highest good, because the first good … All the names of God are comprehended in this one of good.[2]

So, what is goodness? Considering it is found in the very heart and essence of God, attempting a definition is intimidating. At times in theology it is somewhat of an umbrella term: God's love, mercy, long-suffering, and kindness are all manifestations of his goodness. It is the absence of any imperfection or defect, and the presence of perfect wholeness.

---

[1] à Brakel, *The Christian's Reasonable Service*, 1:122.
[2] Stephen Charnock, *Discourses on the Existence and Attributes of God* in *Works* (1864; repr. Edinburgh: Banner of Truth Trust, 2010), 2:280.

Did the ancient philosophers like Plato have it right? Is that something that is transcendental and really belongs only to God? The Bible provides a different answer. While goodness begins and properly belongs with God, it does not stay there. He pours out his goodness and manifests it in tangible ways, not only that we can see, but that we ourselves can manifest as well.

Goodness in Creation and Providence

First, let us consider goodness in creation and providence. As God sets about creating the universe, he ensures that it reflects this aspect of his being. With each subsequent work of creation, God surveys the production and calls it 'good.' This means so much more than simply that God liked it, though he did. The creation is not good in the sense that it is useful to God, though it is. Nor is it good because it is aesthetically pleasing, though it most certainly was and still is. This benediction is saying so much more than that. Apologist Francis Schaeffer says that when God makes this benediction he is essentially saying, 'Every step and every sphere of creation, and the whole thing put together—man himself and his total environment, the heavens and the earth—*conforms to myself.*'[3] The transcendent Good had come into this world—without it there would be no world at all. It was right. It was ordered. It was all very good.

[3] Francis A. Schaeffer, *Genesis in Space and Time: The Flow of Biblical History* (Downers Grove, IL: InterVarsity Press, 1972), p. 55 (emphasis added).

Of course, we know that sin comes in and terribly disrupts this goodness. Where there was at one time peace, there is now disorder. Wrong replaces the right. Not long after God saw that 'it was good' we read that instead he 'saw that the wickedness of man was great in the earth, and that every intention of the thoughts of his heart was only evil continually' (Gen. 6:5).

Yet even so, God continues to inject his goodness into the world through his acts of providence. God's providence is every way in which he continues to sustain and secure this world and those who live in it—that is a *good* thing! The Belgic Confession roots the reality of providence in the attribute of God's goodness: 'We believe this good God, after he created all things, did not abandon them to chance or fortune but leads and governs them according to his holy will, in such a way that nothing happens in this world without his orderly arrangement.'[4]

Providence teaches us that the wrong does not always win out. We see again and again that which is proper, right, and good manifested in the world around us. God continues to act in this world, governing by his essence of goodness. Thus the psalmist extols him: 'You are good and do good' (119:68). Jesus himself explained how God's providential preservation of his creatures was a sign of his goodness. He feeds the sparrows and clothes the field, and he will certainly care for those who ask and seek him: 'If you then, who are evil, know how to

[4] The Belgic Confession, Article 13.

give good gifts to your children, how much more will your Father who is in heaven give good things to those who ask him!' (Matt. 7:11).

The breath you have just taken is a gift from a good God. The reason you are alive today is because God is and does good. And the only proper response is thanksgiving. As we are told time and again in Scripture: 'Give thanks to the Lord, for he is good' (e.g., Ezra 3:11; 1 Chron. 16:34; Psa. 106:1, 107:1, 136:1).

Goodness in Question

And yet thanksgiving is not always the response we have to the goodness of God. Far from it, for many people instead call God's goodness into question altogether. How often have we heard (or perhaps asked ourselves) the question: 'If God is good, how can he allow—?' This is not a new question. It began in the all-good Garden, where Satan gets Eve to doubt the goodness of God: 'Did God really say …? Surely a good God who would create such a good place wouldn't require you to do something that seems so … *not* good.' And the doubting and distrusting of God's goodness has continued up to today, perhaps even reaching a fever pitch in our postmodern era.

The problem of evil and suffering in the world for many is incompatible with the conception of a good, beneficent God. New Atheists, such as Christopher Hitchens and Richard Dawkins, have tossed out God altogether. Others might find themselves more along the lines of French poet Charles Baudelaire, who concluded, 'If there is a God, he is the devil.'[5] Or we come to the same conclusion as young Odie O'Banion, protagonist in William Kent Krueger's bestselling book *This Tender Land*, who, after being orphaned, abused, and losing a loved one to the terror of a tornado, replaces his conception of a good God with one that he titles 'the Tornado God.' Indeed, the unforgiving winds and chaotic, destructive path of a tornado are about as opposite from the property of goodness that one can get.

What is the solution when goodness is called into question like this? On one hand, we must recognize the validity of the observation that bad, even evil, things happen. The innocent are taken advantage of, the vulnerable are abused, the guilty are let off. Wars ravage nations, while sickness and disease and disaster have wiped out entire civilizations. How do we reconcile the presence of evil with the idea of God's goodness? We could say, borrowing C. S. Lewis' assessment of Aslan, 'Course he isn't safe. But he's good.'[6] How can the dangers of this world still uphold the goodness of the King? The answer is found in Jesus Christ.

To have a fully formed conception of what goodness is, you cannot just look to creation, you cannot just look

---

[5] Cited in Francis Schaeffer, *The God Who Is There* (Downers Grove, IL: InterVarsity Press, 1968), p. 100.

[6] Lewis, *The Lion, the Witch, and the Wardrobe*, p. 76.

to providence—you must ultimately look to redemption. Those atheists and cynics who have rejected the God of the Bible because they claim he cannot possibly be good have not taken into proper account the gospel. This is what completes the picture of goodness. Yes, evil exists. And God permits that evil, true enough. But, in the words of Michael Horton, '[God] only actively permits evils that he has already, *at great personal cost*, determined to overcome for his great glory *and our ultimate good*.'[7] That personal cost is the death of his Son, Jesus Christ. And it is because of Jesus Christ we can know with certainty 'that for those who love God all things work together *for good*' (Rom. 8:28, emphasis added).

Goodness in Redemption

How can this be the case? If we return to Jesus' comment to the rich young ruler, we may think that he himself is denying that divine, essential quality of goodness should be applied to him: 'Why do you call me good? No one is good but God alone.' But that is not what Jesus is saying. The title 'good teacher' was not in use by the Jewish people, and never attributed to even the best of rabbis, because they believed goodness to be an attribute belonging only to God. And so, far from denying his goodness, and thereby his deity, he was inviting the ruler to reflect on the meaning of his own words. Charnock writes that

---

[7] Michael S. Horton, *The Christian Faith* (Grand Rapids: Zondervan, 2011), p. 359, emphasis added. Cf. WCF 5.4.

Jesus 'doth not here deny his deity, but reproves [the rich young ruler] for calling him good, when he had not yet confessed him to be *more than* a man ... He disowns not his own deity, but allures the young man to a confession of it.'[8]

By asking 'Why do you call *me* good?' he is forcing the young man to reflect on his own perception of who he was. Unintentionally, this ruler had made an audacious—though entirely accurate—claim about who Jesus was! All of the goodness that is in God is in Jesus Christ as well. Says Puritan Thomas Brooks, 'Christ is the greatest good, the choicest good, the chiefest good, the most suitable good, the most necessary good. He is a pure good, a real good, a total good, an eternal good, and a soul-satisfying good.'[9]

In what ways do we see that supreme goodness in Jesus? It is an important question. In a sense, it is the question Jesus was asking back to the rich young ruler: 'What about me is good? What makes you say that I am good?' If Jesus put the question to you, how would you answer? One important answer—*the* important answer—is that Jesus is good because he obeys, submits to, serves, and fulfils God's law, which is by nature good. 'Your rules are *good*,' says the psalmist (119:39, emphasis added). Paul writes in Romans 7:12, 'So the law is holy, and the commandment is holy and righteous and *good*.' Notice the

[8] Charnock, *Existence and Attributes*, 2:277-278 (emphasis added).
[9] Thomas Brooks, *Precious Remedies Against Satan's Devices* (Edinburgh: Banner of Truth Trust, 1997), p. 221.

close comparison between the ideas of righteousness and goodness: the law is good because it is right, it is proper, it is just. Jesus is good for these very same reasons, too.

He was born 'under the law' (Gal. 4:4), and his life's ministry was not to abolish or break the law but to fulfil it (Matt. 5:17). Jesus points the rich young ruler to the same answer. What does the Good Teacher have to say about what will make for a good life? Look to the Law of God, Jesus says. 'You know the commandments: "Do not commit adultery, Do not murder, Do not steal, Do not bear false witness, Honour your father and mother"' (Luke 18:20). Jesus elsewhere summarizes the law of God like this: 'The most important is, "Hear, O Israel: The Lord our God, the Lord is one. And you shall love the Lord your God with all your heart and with all your soul and with all your mind and with all your strength." The second is this: "You shall love your neighbour as yourself." There is no other commandment greater than these' (Mark 12:29-31).

Our salvation hinges upon the fact that Jesus Christ, in perfect goodness, fulfilled these two great commandments. He always did the right thing. With him there was always completeness and wholeness in his actions before God and others, so Peter could simply say of him to Cornelius, 'He went about *doing good*' (Acts 10:38, emphasis added).

These two great commandments lay before all of us. We are called to this life as well. And yet we have a threshold, do we not? We love God, until another god-like ambition or comfort gets in the way. We love our neighbours ... *up to a point*. We all have a threshold, a limitation on our goodness. But the threshold for Jesus was death. Let's be honest: oftentimes we cap our love because we don't think people are deserving of it. Why should I go to all these lengths to serve or help or forgive someone who makes it his aim in life to offend me? After all, perhaps for *a good* person we might dare even to die. Ah, but God shows his love for us, shows his goodness to us, in that while we were not good at all, while we were still sinners, Christ died for us (Rom. 5:8).

This is why in his great discourse in John 10, Jesus says he loves and cares for us not just like any shepherd, but as the *good* shepherd 'who lays down his life for the sheep' (verse 11). It was his goodness, his conviction of doing the right thing, that took him to the cross. 'The whole gospel is nothing but one entire mirror of divine goodness,' wrote Charnock.[10] Do you see it?

The Good Shepherd not only lays down his life, but he takes it back up again (verse 17). It's the resurrection that completes the Good News of the gospel, and which fills in the picture of true Goodness. When we take all of redemption into account, the questions and doubts about God's goodness start to have an answer. The evil that has entered this world does not get the final say. For the wickedness of man Jesus dies, and for the security

[10] Charnock, *Existence and Attributes*, 2:317.

of our eternal happiness in the presence of the only true Good, God himself, Jesus lives again.

Goodness in Me

We have seen goodness in creation and providence, we have seen goodness in Christ, and yet there is one more place we must see it: in ourselves. 'Now wait a minute,' you may be thinking. 'Hasn't Jesus already established that none is good besides God?' He has. And it is true: ever since the Fall none of us share in that pure goodness with which God made the world. It is broken, ruptured. As Paul says, quoting the psalms, 'None is righteous, no, not one; no one understands; no one seeks for God. All have turned aside; together they have become worthless; no one does good, not even one' (Rom. 3:10-12). But conversion changes all of that.

When we put our faith in Jesus Christ, he takes us out of this broken and fallen world, as it were, and places us into the pure, eternal realm of God's goodness (Col. 1:13, 14). Our natures change. The Apostle John tells us, 'Whoever does good is from God; whoever does evil has not seen God,' and because of this new Spirit-birthed reality in our hearts we are to 'not imitate evil but imitate good' (3 John 11).

Knowing Jesus and being united to him transforms us and gives us a capacity for goodness. Being made right with God will make our hearts right. We will be able to live and love in ways that are good, wholesome, and true. Psalm 25:8 says, 'Good and upright is the LORD; therefore he instructs sinners in the way.' Because God is good and righteous, through Jesus Christ he aims to make us good and righteous as well. George Bethune sums it up well—again tying the ideas of goodness and righteousness together—when he says, '[God's] goodness, combined with his love of righteousness, moves him to make sinners happy by making them holy.'[11]

Of course, conversion won't make us perfectly good. Glorification does that. We are not completely in the realm of God: we have one foot there, and one foot here. Paul himself struggles with his weak endeavours to be good in this life: 'For I know that nothing good dwells in me, that is, in my flesh. For I have the desire to do what is right, but not the ability to carry it out. For I do not do the good I want, but the evil I do not want is what I keep on doing' (Rom. 7:18, 19).

We will all have those weak moments. The way to overcome them is not to try to *do* more; it is to *believe* more. It is to endeavour seriously after those foundational Christian rhythms of faith and repentance. We must rest more in Christ, trusting in the finished work of the cross and the 'good work' of sanctification that he is bringing to completion (Phil. 1:6). As Christians, remember that you only are a fruit-bearing branch as you are united to the Vine. If we look to ourselves to produce goodness and righteousness in our own strength, we will despair.

---

[11] Bethune, *The Fruits of the Spirit*, p. 161.

With Paul, we must find hope outside of ourselves: 'Who will deliver me from this body of death? Thanks be to God through Jesus Christ our Lord!' (Rom. 7:24, 25). Jesus is the answer. If you want to be good you need to be converted. Put down the self-help books. Quit looking for shortcuts and life hacks. Cease the striving. Look to Jesus. Could it be that simple?

When Philip first encountered Jesus it was life-changing. He knew there was something different about this man. He was so excited about his new Master that he went and told his friend Nathaniel to come and follow. But Nathaniel mocks the idea by saying, 'Can anything good come out of Nazareth?' (John 1:46). We could in a sense share that ancient disdain and scepticism: could Jesus really be the solution? Could he be the one that takes my wicked heart and makes it produce something that's truly good?

To that, dear friend, I give you the answer and invitation that Philip gave Nathaniel: 'Come and see.'

7

FAITHFUL TO HIM WHO
APPOINTED HIM

COMPELLED by a sense of duty, and convinced that his mission is too dangerous for the rest of his company, at the conclusion of *The Fellowship of the Ring* Frodo Baggins determines he must set off to destroy the One Ring all on his own. He leaves without saying a word, hoping to slip away unnoticed by his friends. And yet he cannot get past his dearest companion, Samwise Gamgee. As Sam pleads for his friend not to leave without him, Frodo gives Sam a sobering account of the journey ahead, assuming this will deter him:

'I am going to Mordor,' he says.

Without hesitation, Sam replies, 'I know that well enough, Mr Frodo. Of course you are. And I'm coming with you.'

After some arguing back and forth, Frodo finally relents: 'It is no good trying to escape you. But I'm glad,

Sam. I cannot tell you how glad. Come along! It is plain that we were meant to go together.'[1]

The story of a friend like Samwise warms our hearts. But is such faithfulness only found in the realm of fiction? After all, King Solomon laments in Proverbs, 'A faithful man who can find?' (20:6). The kind of devotion and long-term loyalty—even in the face of danger—that Tolkien gave us in the character of Sam are traits that are hard to come by.

But thanks be to God, there is a faithful friend for all of us in the person of Jesus. He is marked by faithfulness to his Father, and faithfulness to us. That means his faithfulness is not something we merely read about; it is something we experience. He never will give up on us, no matter what trials lay ahead. United everlastingly by his Spirit, it is of Jesus we can truly say, 'It is plain that we were meant to go together!' This quality of faithfulness is one of the very reasons why the author of Hebrews says we are to look to Jesus: 'Therefore, holy brothers, you who share in a heavenly calling, consider Jesus, the apostle and high priest of our confession, who was faithful to him who appointed him' (3:1, 2).

[1] J. R. R. Tolkien, *The Fellowship of the Ring: Being the first part of The Lord of the Rings* (New York: Houghton Mifflin Company, 1994), p. 397.

The 'What' of Christ's Faithfulness

One of the reasons we should think on Jesus, and one of the reasons he should matter to us at all, is because he is that rare example of true faithfulness. He committed himself to undertake that to which God appointed him. He fulfilled his mission. The faithfulness referred to here in Hebrews is the same faithfulness Paul had in mind with the seventh fruit of the Spirit. It is not the fruit of belief—this is not referring to our ability to believe.[2] In a sense it is the opposite of that: it is the fruit that makes you a person *worth believing in.* You are loyal, true, trustworthy, you keep your commitments, your bond, so that people can put their faith *in* you. 'The faithful person is reliable for important tasks, loyal to friends, and dependable in emergencies.'[3] And if there was ever a person worthy of our faith, over and above all others, it is Jesus Christ.

The opening chapters of Hebrews argue the 'greater than-ness' of Jesus. He is greater than angels, greater than priests, greater than sacrifices. According to Hebrews 3:2, one of the things that makes Jesus so great, even greater than Moses, is that he was faithful. We read, 'He was faithful to him who appointed him, just as Moses also was faithful in all God's house. For Jesus has been

[2] If you are reading from the Authorised (King James) Version you may be tempted to think this, since that translation reads 'The fruit of the Spirit is … faith.'

[3] Philip Graham Ryken, *Galatians* (Phillipsburg, NJ: P&R, 2005), p. 233.

counted worthy of more glory than Moses—as much more glory as the builder of a house has more honour than the house itself' (3:2, 3). Moses was faithful. God says this himself in Numbers when he extols him over other Israelite prophets: 'He is faithful in all my house' (12:7). Yet his faithfulness is but a shadow of the real thing which is seen in Jesus Christ. Jesus is greater and more glorious than Moses because he is more faithful: his mission was more difficult, more significant, and he took it on with no misgivings (unlike Moses; Exod. 3:11) and carried it out perfectly to the end (again, unlike Moses; Num. 20:12).

What was this mission that Jesus accomplished? It was the mission of redemption, of course, carried out through his perfect, law-fulfiling life, and selfless, curse-bearing death.

That is the big picture of it. But we are given a zoomed-in, more detailed account of Christ's mission in John 17, the passage known as the High Priestly Prayer. In this moving scene hours before his betrayal and arrest, the Son cries out to the Father in a passionate prayer that he would be glorified and the elect would be saved. Jesus declares, 'I glorified you on earth, having accomplished the work that you gave me to do' (verse 4). As we examine the remainder of this magnificent prayer, we note three aspects of *what* Christ did that proves his faithfulness to you and me.

He manifested God's name

First, he manifested God's name. 'I have manifested your name to the people whom you gave me out of the world' (verse 6). 'While I was with them, I kept them in your name, which you have given me' (verse 12). 'I made known to them your name, and I will continue to make it known, that the love with which you have loved me may be in them, and I in them' (verse 26). <u>God's name is Yahweh, the great I AM WHAT I AM. His name is his being and essence: the holy, eternal, everlasting, self-sufficient, all-glorious God</u>. For Moses, that name was manifested in a burning-but-not-burnt bush. But now the name, the very nature of God, is manifested in the person of Jesus Christ. And not just to one individual, but to the whole world—savingly so, 'to the people whom you gave me out of the world,' as Jesus says in verse 6.

Apart from God manifesting himself to us, revealing himself to us, we could never know him. He is transcendent and quite literally out of this world. Our finite minds cannot comprehend the infinite. But God chooses to reveal himself in a way that we can understand, in a way that we get—in flesh and blood. So the Apostle says, 'No one has ever seen God; the only God, who is at the Father's side, he has made him known' (John 1:18). <u>Jesus has been faithful to God by perfectly representing God. When we look into the face of Christ, we see God.</u>

He preached God's word

Second, Jesus shows his faithfulness in that he preached the words of life. 'I have given them the words that you gave me' (John 17:8). His mission was accomplished in part because, as he says in this prayer, 'I have given them your word' (verse 14). This is no easy thing, because the world naturally hates the words and things of God. Verse 14 goes on: 'I have given them your word, and the world has hated them because they are not of the world, just as I am not of the world.' It is hard to do the right thing when the right thing is not popular. That is when many of us cave. Why be the lone dissenter? Why draw that kind of unwanted attention? Jesus did not break under the pressure, though. He was faithful in preaching the truth that leads to eternal life, even though it made the masses want to silence him, even kill him, all the more (John 5:18).

He kept God's people

Third, Jesus is faithful to the mission of redemption because he kept and guarded his people. 'While I was with them, I kept them in your name, which you have given me. I have guarded them, and not one of them has been lost except the son of destruction, that the Scripture might be fulfilled' (John 17:12). In fact, this third aspect is fulfilled in the first two. As one scholar puts it, 'During his ministry Jesus kept the disciples safe in the revelation of the Father embodied in Jesus himself so that they did not turn aside from it.'[4] He continually comforted and convicted them of the truth so that they did not fall away. Christ is a keeper. His character is that of a steadfast friend, who never lets his loved ones go.

And it should be noted that through the ministry of his Spirit, Jesus continues to do the same for believers today—all because he completed his mission. Those opening words of the prayer should fill the believer's heart with joy and thanksgiving: 'I glorified you on earth, *having accomplished the work* that you gave me to do' (emphasis added). None of us can perfectly accomplish the work God gives us. Therefore we have no hope unless we hope in Christ. As J. C. Ryle says, 'He has finished the work of redemption, and wrought out a perfect righteousness for his people. Unlike the first Adam, who failed to do God's will and brought sin into the world, the second Adam has done all, and left nothing undone that he came to do.'[5]

Objection(s)!

At some point or another, questions will almost certainly creep into the sin-stricken and doubting heart of the Christian regarding the faithfulness of Jesus. The first is this: *Are there conditions?* That is, what qualifications do I need to meet in order to receive his steadfast love? What

[4] Colin G. Kruse, *John* in Tyndale New Testament Commentaries (Downers Grove, IL: InterVarsity, 2003), p. 337.

[5] J. C. Ryle, *Expository Thoughts on the Gospel of John* (Edinburgh: Banner of Truth Trust, 2012), p. 127.

is the fine print to Jesus' faithfulness? We have all been rejected by people we thought we could trust or hope in. Will Jesus turn me away because I do not meet some list of prerequisites that make me worthy of experiencing his faithfulness?

Foreseeing our weak faith, Jesus pre-emptively answers this question for us when he boldly and freely declares, 'Whoever comes to me I will never cast out' (John 6:37). It is this promise of the faithful Saviour, and not any promise of faith we could ever make, that qualifies us to receive his unfailing love. So, dear sinner, know this: the only condition to benefit from the faithfulness of Christ is to receive it. In the words of hymnwriter Joseph Hart,

> Let not conscience make you linger,
> Nor of fitness fondly dream;
> All the fitness he requireth
> Is to feel your need of him.[6]

A second nagging, worrying question about the faithfulness of Jesus is similar: *Is there an extent or limit to it?* Once I receive it, can I lose it? Does his faithfulness have an expiration date? Can it be outdone? Will it be there tomorrow? Can I rely on it all the time and anytime? Can I weary the faithfulness of Jesus Christ?

The gloriously freeing gospel truth is that even 'if we are faithless, he remains faithful' (2 Tim. 2:13). The Old Testament equivalent of this verse is Malachi 3:6, 'For I

---

[6] Joseph Hart, 'Come Ye Sinners, Poor and Needy', 1759.

the LORD do not change; therefore you, O children of Jacob, are not consumed.' God has promised salvation to those who look to Jesus. And he does not renege on his promises. Because he is not like us, because he is not fickle and does not change his mind, we can rest assured of our salvation. Otherwise, he would have destroyed us long ago because of the ways we have betrayed him and sinned against him. But because he does not change, because he is faithful, we are not consumed.

In this way, we start to see how the faithfulness of God in Christ Jesus cannot be measured. As he is infinite in his being, so he is infinite in his commitment to you. 'Your steadfast love, O LORD, extends to the heavens, your faithfulness to the clouds' (Psa. 36:5). 'Your faithfulness endures to all generations' (Psa. 119:90). This faithfulness is so manifest in Jesus Christ that when he comes again in glory the whole world will herald him as the One who is called 'Faithful and True' (Rev. 19:11).

He is not going anywhere, dear Christian. His faithfulness is as an ocean without brim or bottom. It is as high as heaven, as long as eternity, and as big as God himself. Jesus goes with us all the way. He never leaves our side. The moment of soul-cheering assurance comes for the Christian when you can say, 'It is plain that we were meant to go together!' He never is distracted, has to take another appointment, grows weary, or gives up. His is a love that truly never fails (1 Cor. 13:8). If you are ever worried that Jesus might fail you like that one spouse, or business partner, or former friend, take to heart these words: 'Jesus Christ is the same yesterday and today and *forever*' (Heb. 13:8, emphasis added).

The 'So What?' of Christ's Faithfulness

So where do we go from that glorious reality? What is our response to this faithfulness? In one sense it is quite simple: in gratitude we are to be faithful, too.

Jesus calls us to follow him, and what he wants is no half-hearted effort. He wants all of us, all of the time: 'No one who puts his hand to the plough and looks back is fit for the kingdom of God' (Luke 9:62). We cannot turn away. If it sounds daunting, be encouraged that the very same Spirit who anointed Jesus to accomplish his mission from God is the Spirit that lives in you. What a marvel! This means not only *can* you cultivate a life of faithfulness, but you *will* cultivate a life of faithfulness. In doing so, consider that we must first prioritize a faithfulness to the Lord, and from that will flow a faithfulness to others.

First, examine your faithfulness to God, which is what God wants from us above all else. Are you committed to spending time with him in worship, private and family devotions, and prayer? Are you willing to submit to his direction in your life, no matter how difficult that might be? It is easy to be a Christian around other Christians, but faithfulness to Christ is formed in the world, and forged on the anvil of time and opposition. Faithfulness means sticking with the gospel even when the world wants you to abandon it. A university professor once boasted, 'One of my callings in life is to shatter the faith of naive fundamentalists as they come to my class. Just give me a room of young, naive evangelicals and let me at 'em. You can just watch them drop like flies hit with [a swatter] when I challenge their faith in a deliberate, consistent manner.'[7]

In the ancient world, in a time when it was much harder to be a Christian than it is in the West today, the apostles recognized how important this perseverance was. Timothy was known as a 'faithful child in the Lord' (1 Cor. 4:17), and Tychicus a 'faithful minister and fellow servant' (Col. 4:7). Silvanus, according to Peter, is a 'faithful brother' (1 Pet. 5:12), and Gaius is commended by John as being faithful 'in all [his] efforts' for the brothers (3 John 5). At the end of your earthly life, will you be able to look back and know you stood for what was right? Will you have stood with Christ? Will you be able to say with Paul, 'I have fought the good fight, I have finished the race, I have kept the faith' (2 Tim. 4:7)?

Above all, God wants us to be faithful to him. But one of the ways we show that is by faithfulness to the people he has set in our lives, particularly our family and our church. In other words, you do not need to look far at all to find areas in your life calling for your devotion. J. V. Fesko writes, 'God's people should also be marked

---

[7] In Charles R. Swindoll, *Swindoll's Ultimate Book of Illustrations & Quotes* (Nashville, TN: Thomas Nelson, 1998), p. 195.

by a faithfulness, a loyalty, to the church. When so many things in life compete for our loyalty and faithfulness, it is Christ, our families, and the church that should top the list—all else is secondary.'[8]

So, are you a faithful spouse? Perhaps you are not having an illicit relationship with another individual, but the X-rated browsing history on your computer or phone betrays your infidelity.

Are you being a faithful parent? Perhaps you have not abandoned your kids to a child support cheque once a month, but do they see more of you or their favourite character on TV? Are you available for them? Are they more important than your work email? Can they count on you?

Are you a faithful friend? Maybe so, since you are always down to hang out and chat, but why are you not available when your friend needs help?

Are you a faithful church member? Your spotless attendance would suggest yes, but your prayer life devoid of intercession for fellow members says otherwise.

We must always bear in mind, however, that as Christians there is not a single aspect of our life where we are exempt from faithfulness. Therefore, we must carefully audit our various callings and relationships. Where we have fallen short, we must repent and recommit ourselves to reflecting the faithful Saviour, solely by relying on the Spirit's work in our hearts. You are never too young in life,

[8] Fesko, *The Fruit of the Spirit Is …*, p. 56.

or too new in Christ, to begin. Start being a dependable person now by being faithful in the small things in life. Do your chores. Complete the tasks given you. Be on time. If you say you are going to do something, do it. There is no shame in menial tasks when they are accomplished well. In fact, there is only great gain! When you are faithful in the little things in your life, Jesus promises to reward you with much, in this life and ultimately in the next (Matt. 25:21).

How many hours are left in your week right now? There are only so many things you can give yourself to. Give yourself to Jesus. Give yourself entirely unto the One who has given all of himself to you. That Christ-centredness will create a character in you that is devoted to others, dependable, trustworthy, true, and faithful.

8

'I AM GENTLE'

'YOU'RE invited!' Don't you just love getting that card in the mail? Of all the cards to get, an invitation card is the most exciting. Whether it's a wedding, a graduation, or a birthday, we love to be included. The nicer the invite, the grander the party promises to be! It fills you with anticipation. Well, when you open up Matthew 11:28-30, you are opening up the greatest invitation in the world. One that comes from the Saviour of the world himself, addressed right to you.

> Come to me, all who labour and are heavy laden, and I will give you rest. Take my yoke upon you, and learn from me, for I am gentle and lowly in heart, and you will find rest for your souls. For my yoke is easy, and my burden is light.

What is Jesus inviting us to? He is inviting us to have rest. Not a nap, but relief from our greatest distress and burdens. The invitation is for those who are 'weary and heavy laden.' Jesus is not zeroing in on a few people who might be particularly overwhelmed by their calling in life or overcome by the trials they are facing. He is referring to every single one of us, because the weariness and burden that he speaks of is the one caused by sin. None of us is exempt from that trouble, and so the invitation is a universal one. More than being a universal offer, it is an efficacious offer. Jesus not only recognizes our need, but he has the very thing that can meet that need: rest. Rest here is a synonym for salvation. It is the promise of heaven when what we deserve is hell.

Why does he make such an offer? Why not leave us to our sin? We ought to be condemned. We are traitors and rebels. We do not deserve anything but God's wrath. But Jesus comes as that manifestation of the character of God who, according to Psalm 103:10, 'does not deal with us as our sins deserve, or repay us according to our iniquities.' Our sins deserve God's harsh—but just—wrath. Yet instead of this, we receive his gentleness in Jesus.

Two Characteristics

This whole study has been an examination of the character of Christ. So far we have taken a look into his loving, joyful, patient, peaceful, kind, good, and faithful heart. But did you know that this is the only place in all of Scripture where Jesus actually describes the nature of his own heart?[1] This line in Matthew 11:29 is the only

---

[1] Ortlund, *Gentle and Lowly*, p. 17.

time where Christ actually says, 'Let me tell you about my heart.' And what does he say? What is his own self-assessment of his nature and disposition? That he is *gentle*! Out of all of the fruits of the Spirit, gentleness is the only one that Jesus explicitly attributes to himself in this way. It is as though he were to say, 'If you want to know me, know that I am gentle.' That in and of itself should cause us to lean forward in our seats to learn what gentleness is all about. In so doing, we will also take into account the complementary attribute of lowliness.

Gentleness

How do you handle something that is fragile? When I was a child, my class did a project where we competed to see which of us could construct the best container for protecting an egg. We had several days to work at home experimenting and putting our device together, and then came the moment of truth: whose egg could survive a drop from the classroom's first-storey window? The survivors advanced to the next floor, and then the next, until only one egg remained. Admittedly, it is a bizarre experiment when you think about it: recognizing the fragility of the egg, we worked hard to invent something that would protect it, something gentle—but then we did the least gentle thing imaginable and tossed it out a window!

Gentleness is handling something that is fragile according to its nature, so that it does not break, so that there is not even the *threat* of it breaking. When the Greek word from Galatians 5 or Matthew 11 is used elsewhere in the New Testament, the authors are acknowledging our fragile human nature. They recognize that when we interact with one another, even when (and especially when) people are frustrating us or have hurt us, it is incumbent upon us to respond with gentleness:

> 'Brothers, if anyone is caught in any transgression, you who are spiritual should restore him in a spirit of gentleness.' (Gal. 6:1)

> 'The Lord's servant must not be quarrelsome but kind to everyone, able to teach, patiently enduring evil, correcting his opponents with gentleness.' (2 Tim. 2:24, 25)

> 'What do you wish? Shall I come to you with a rod, or with love in a spirit of gentleness?' (1 Cor. 4:21)

> 'I therefore, a prisoner for the Lord, urge you to walk in a manner worthy of the calling to which you have been called, with all humility and gentleness, with patience, bearing with one another in love' (Eph. 4:1, 2)

We are so fragile that a harsh word or a cruel look is enough to break our spirits. That is the way the world treats us. So Jesus invites us to himself, to experience something we have never fully experienced before: perfect gentleness. Having a fallen, finite human nature is like being dressed in a 'handle with care' label, a label that the world ignores and therefore tosses us around—but

God in Jesus Christ 'gently bears us.'[2] He embodies the fulfilment of all of those New Testament imperatives. He is not reactionary in rage toward us. He does not push us beyond our limits. In his wonderful treatment of this subject, Dane Ortlund says that this word teaches us that Jesus is 'the most understanding person in the universe. The posture most natural to him is not a pointed finger but open arms.'[3]

The prophet Isaiah predicted the gentleness of Jesus (and Matthew confirms it), when he wrote of the coming servant of God: 'a bruised reed he will not break, and a faintly burning wick he will not quench' (Isa. 42:3; cf. Matt. 12:15-21). He does not stomp on a tender piece of grass, or snuff out a flickering candle. He does not take delight in crushing that which is small and weak and helpless.

But it is not that Jesus simply avoids hurting that which is fragile; he is drawn to *help* it. Generally people have two reactions when they see a newborn baby that is not their own. One reaction is to be threatened by the smallness and helplessness of the baby. These people do not want to hold the baby because they are afraid of doing something wrong and accidentally hurting it. Others see that same child and have the opposite reaction: the helplessness of the baby draws them to it, and they want to hold it, to cradle it in their arms. Precisely *because* it

---

[2] Henry F. Lyte, 'Praise, My Soul, the King of Heaven', 1834.
[3] Ortlund, *Gentle and Lowly*, p. 19.

is weak and delicate, they want to protect and cherish it. Which reaction does Jesus have when he looks upon us and our frailties? He is drawn to us. The Puritan Richard Sibbes, in his devotional classic *The Bruised Reed*, writes that 'he will not only not break nor quench, but he will cherish those with whom he so deals.'[4] This is the gentleness of Jesus.

Lowliness

Jesus says something else about his heart in this passage, doesn't he? He is gentle *and lowly* in heart. The two ideas work closely together. The word here implies an association with the low or despised social classes. In other places it is translated 'to be humbled.' Jesus' lowliness is precisely *how* he is gentle. He comes down to us and meets us where we are. He empathizes with us. When we come to Jesus we can be assured of his gentleness because we are not simply running into the arms of a god, which would be terrifying and would consume us. Rather, when we come to Jesus we are running into the arms of the God *who became man*. He associates with us so much that he became us.

Jesus is lowly in that he came low to the earth. He condescended from his heavenly heights of grandeur and took the form of a servant (Phil. 2:5-8). He quite literally exchanged the high realm of heaven for the low places of

[4] Richard Sibbes, *The Bruised Reed* (Edinburgh: Banner of Truth Trust, 2008), p. 7.

this earth and our sad condition. <u>Since he is lowly, he is equipped and prepared and perfectly suited to serve us in gentleness.</u>

The lowliness of Jesus teaches the accessibility of Jesus. When he says 'come to me,' you can really, truly go to him. He is available. He is ready and eager to meet with you. And because he is at our level, so to speak, the yoke he will place upon us will not be one we cannot bear.

A yoke was the heavy wooden contraption worn by oxen that kept them moving in unison as they ploughed a field. People would also wear yokes to help them balance weighty loads across their shoulders, when they would carry water, for example. Yokes were useful, but they were heavy. But because Jesus is lowly, at our level, and knows our weakness, he gives us a yoke we can actually carry without wearying. In fact, what Jesus gives his followers is less a burden than it is a buoy—something that keeps us afloat rather than weighing us down. Those who are willing to submit to the instruction and lordship of Christ will find themselves uplifted, for 'the LORD lifts up the humble' (Psa. 147:6).

An Imperative

In this passage, beyond describing his heart, Jesus gives an imperative: 'Learn from me.' We are to learn the way of gentleness and lowliness from Christ, discovering how to approach that which is fragile with the tender care of our Saviour. Our world has some terrible misconceptions about gentleness. One misconception would be that it is weakness. This idea says that anytime we do not show force, we are conceding inability. Gentleness is despised in the political system of every nation, where powerful posturing seems to be the most critical component of statecraft. But gentleness is not the absence of power; it is the proper use of it—not to crush or destroy or dismay, but to protect and build up. Think again of Jesus with the bruised reed. Matthew Henry wrote of that passage: 'He will not break the bruised reed, but will strengthen it, that it may become a cedar in the courts of our God. He will not quench the faintly burning wick, but blow it up into a flame.'[5] That takes power. If we don't recognize that things like gentleness, humility, and meekness are born out of power, then we will easily confuse them with non-virtues such as timidity or cowardice.[6]

So, dear Christian, learn from Jesus Christ what real gentleness is. It is coming to people that you know are innately fragile and must be handled with care. Jesus comes to his people 'humble, and mounted on a donkey' (Matt. 21:5)—the word translated 'humble' is the same as 'gentle' in this text and in Galatians 5. It is the idea of not flaunting yourself, your personality, your prowess, or your power. And we have seen it is intimately connected with the idea of lowliness, too. The fruit of gentleness that

---

[5] Matthew Henry, *Commentary on the Whole Bible* (Peabody, MA: Hendrickson, 1996), 4:179.
[6] Bridges, *The Fruitful Life*, p. 122.

the Spirit will cultivate in the lives of believers will come in tandem with this attribute of lowliness, of humility and accessibility. It is the gentle soul that can adhere to Paul's instructions in Romans 12:16, 'Live in harmony with one another. Do not be haughty, but associate with the lowly.'

Are you on your high horse? Gentleness is found nearer the ground. Cultivate this fruit by living a life of accessibility to all people from all walks of life, and never think yourself better or more important than anyone.

A proper sense of our own sin will cause us to handle with care the weak, sorrowing, or difficult sinners around us. We need that broken and contrite heart that God will never despise (Psa. 51:17). To know the tender way that God has dealt with our sin, and to believe the unchanging reality of our justification and right standing before the Judge, will give us what we need to deal carefully, compassionately, and gently with others. Jonathan Edwards says that the Christian who is touched by his need and infirmity 'has the firmest comfort, but the softest heart: richer than others, but poorest of all in spirit. He is the tallest and strongest saint, but the least and tenderest child among them.'[7]

Is that not what it is to 'learn from' Jesus? As we are told in Philippians, Jesus, 'though he was in the form of God, did not count equality with God a thing to be grasped, but emptied himself, by taking the form of a

---

[7] Jonathan Edwards, *Religious Affections*, in *Works*, 1:309.

servant, being born in the likeness of men' (2:6, 7). There is a call here for us to examine our lives in light of who Jesus is. Do you think you are better than others? Has this led to harshness or impatience? Are you quick-tempered? Do you care little about the sensitivities of those around you? Are you concerned primarily with getting your way rather than accommodating the needs of others? If so, then you must look to this gentle Saviour and learn gentleness!

An Invitation

But note well that the imperative rightly only comes after the invitation.[8] The 'learn from me' can only happen *after* the 'come to me.' So, again, dear fragile sinner: come to your gentle Saviour. Knowing that Jesus will not break the bruised, or quench the fainthearted, you have every reason to come to him. We have every reason to run to him and 'with confidence draw near to the throne of grace' (Heb. 4:16). We have every reason because, due to sin, we *are* the bruised and faint—the very people that Jesus welcomes!

Ah, but you still hesitate. You are still uncertain. We established at the beginning of the chapter that Matthew

---

[8] I have found these two terms helpful in considering all commands in Scripture. When God gives us an imperative, it is really an invitation out of ourselves and into a world of holiness and happiness. Likewise, when he gives us an invitation, the converted will understand it is nothing other than an imperative: there is no proper way to respond but to accept.

11:29 is particularly interesting because it is the only place in all of Scripture where Jesus addresses explicitly the nature of his heart. Why is it that gentleness receives special attention from Christ when describing his character? It ties back to this great invitation. He knows our initial, natural reaction as sinners encountering a holy God: it is to shrink away in fear. It is to not come at all. Thomas Goodwin says that 'we are apt to think that he, being so holy, is therefore of a severe and sour disposition against sinners, and not able to bear them. No, says he; "I am meek," gentleness is my nature and temper.' Even his exaltation and ascension cannot change the heart of our Saviour:

> Yea, but (may we think) he being the Son of God and heir of heaven, and especially being now filled with glory, and sitting at God's right hand, he may now despise the lowliness of us here below; though not out of anger, yet out of that height of his greatness and distance that he is advanced unto, in that we are too mean for him to marry, or be familiar with. He surely hath higher thoughts than to regard such poor, low things as we are. And so though indeed we conceive him meek, and not prejudiced with injuries, yet he may be too high and lofty to condescend so far as to regard, or take to heart, the condition of poor creatures. No, says Christ; 'I am lowly' also, willing to bestow my love and favour upon the poorest and meanest.[9]

[9] Goodwin, *The Heart of Christ*, p. 47.

The heights of heaven cannot change the heart of Jesus which set upon the lowly. 'We have our own flesh in heaven as a sure pledge that Christ our head will also take us, his members, up to himself.'[10] How can he forget those whose human nature he still wears? And, as Goodwin also reminds us, the very same Spirit of gentleness that anointed Christ upon earth is with him in glory:

> If the same Spirit that was upon him, and in him, when he was on earth, does but still rest upon him now he is in heaven, then these dispositions must needs still entirely remain in him. ... It must never be said, the Spirit of the Lord is departed from him, who is the sender and bestower of the Holy Spirit upon us. ... [Therefore] 'meekness' is not far off, but is made one of his dispositions in his height of glory.[11]

So, dear sinner, you have every reason to go to gentle Jesus today. And for all your harshness, outbursts of anger, fits of rage, callousness, he will bring you to himself. And having you, he will do something remarkable: he will conform you. He will take a bruised reed and make it a mighty cedar. He will fan into fire the faint flame that is the Spirit's work in your heart. And you will become holy as he is holy, loving as he is loving, and gentle as he is gentle.

Need help in getting started? Why not begin with this prayer:

[10] The Heidelberg Catechism, Q. 49.
[11] Goodwin, *Heart of Christ*, pp. 50, 54, 56.

Gracious Spirit, dwell with me:
I myself would gracious be;
And with words that help and heal
Would thy life in mine reveal;
And with actions bold and meek
Would for Christ my Saviour speak.[12]

---

[12] Thomas T. Lynch, 'Gracious Spirit, Dwell with Me', 1855.

9

'NOT MY WILL
BUT YOURS BE DONE'

Do you feel like you have your life under control, or is the chaos and confusion creeping in and starting to take over? We have all felt like we are losing a grip on our lives at some point or another. Life loves to throw us curveballs: whether it is the disruption of roadwork, a last-minute cancellation, an unexpected bill in the mail, the inconvenience of having your car in the shop, or the maddening attempts to have a phone meeting while also controlling a barking dog and a hyperactive toddler.

We want to have order in our worlds, under-standably. But the Bible never commands us to control our circumstances, but only to control ourselves. To control our circumstances would be an overly ambitious achievement—one that belongs properly to God himself. So many of our problems in life arise from trying to control things we cannot (like our circumstances) and failing to control that which we can (ourselves). Self-control *is* actually achievable—though seemingly just as daunting a task.

What It Is

So, what is it? Self-control has at times been referred to as *temperance*—I think a helpful modern-day synonym would be *discipline*. It is the ability to control our wants, our urges, our emotions and speech. One pastor says that self-control 'manages the operation centre of the believer's heart.'[1] The self-controlled individual isn't a glutton, but can manage their appetite. The self-controlled individual doesn't fly off the handle in a furious rage every time something doesn't go their way—they have mastery over their emotions. Sometimes the things we have to curb or control aren't bad things; it's just that there are *better* things in store if we wait. Is it wrong to check a text message on your phone? No. But self-control will tell you it's better to do it when you're not driving. Self-control will keep our hands on the wheel and our eyes on the road in life, not allowing us to become distracted by our impulses from what really matters.

Self-control was famously tested at Stanford University in the 1960s by psychologist Walter Mischel. Mischel's experiment is commonly known today as the marshmallow test. A single marshmallow is placed in front of a three- or four-year-old, and they are told they are free to

[1] Stanley D. Gale, *A Vine-Ripened Life*, p. 134.

eat the marshmallow now if they want to. But the experimenter also lets them know if they wait just a moment as the experimenter steps outside the room, they can have two when they return. You can see the wheels spinning in these little kids' heads, as they actually squirm in their seats waiting for the experimenter to return. One marshmallow now is great, they are telling themselves. But two marshmallows later is better … or is it? That is the intense struggle these children are going through!

But this experiment helps illustrate the definition of self-control, one we will return to throughout this study. <u>Self-control is the power to wait on a perceived good or withhold present desire, with the knowledge of a guaranteed 'better' in the future.</u>

Notice that I wrote self-control is a 'power.' All the fruits of the Spirit go together, but <u>gentleness and self-control are closely related to one another.</u> And as we learned in the previous chapter, no matter what the world might say, gentleness is not weakness. Refraining from showing force does not make someone weak. Self-control is the same way. In fact, the Greek word used in Galatians literally means 'inner power'—*egkrateia*, from *en* for 'inner' and *kratos* for 'power.' We hear *kratos* in our English word demo*cratic*, which means *power* of the people. Likewise, the ability to show calm amidst the storms of life is truly a display of power.

There is a story told about the soldier, spy, and statesman Sir Walter Raleigh, and how he was once insolently treated by a hot-headed, rash youth who challenged him, and spat in his face when Raleigh refused. Raleigh pulled out his handkerchief and calmly wiped the spit from his face, and made only this reply: 'Young man, if I could as easily wipe your blood from my conscience as I can this injury from my face, I would at this moment take away your life.' While the onlookers might have been terrifyingly impressed if the knight had pulled out his sword and dispatched this fool, it was this response that was the real display of power. It was so powerful, in fact, that the young man was struck with a sense of his improper behaviour and immediately fell on his knees begging forgiveness. Raleigh waited on the perceived good of vengeance because he trusted in the guarantee of a better good in the future: namely, a clean conscience.

Why We Need It

Why do we need this inner power? Why do we need to control ourselves? Why not just listen to every little voice in our heads, bow to every impulse, and satisfy every want? The reason is because the voices in our heads hardly ever know what they are talking about, because our impulses are so often impure, and because our wants are often wicked. In a word, the reason we need self-control is because of sin. The Fall was itself a lack of self-control. The inner power was abused, or neglected entirely.

Go back to the Garden with me. What do we have? We have Satan as the serpent tempting Eve to be like

God. The arena of temptation is where self-control is most needed. And how does he tempt her? He plays upon her desires.

> He said to the woman, 'Did God actually say, "You shall not eat of any tree in the garden"?' And the woman said to the serpent, 'We may eat of the fruit of the trees in the garden, but God said, "You shall not eat of the fruit of the tree that is in the midst of the garden, neither shall you touch it, lest you die."' But the serpent said to the woman, 'You will not surely die. For God knows that when you eat of it your eyes will be opened, and you will be like God, knowing good and evil.' So when the woman saw that the tree was good for food, and that it was a delight to the eyes, and that the tree was to be desired to make one wise, she took of its fruit and ate, and she also gave some to her husband who was with her, and he ate.—Gen. 3:1-6

She saw that the fruit was 'good for food'—it would fill the cravings of her appetite. It was 'a delight to the eyes'—the forbidden fruit allured her aesthetically. But ultimately it was 'desired to make one wise'—Eve wanted the fruit because she wanted to act on the impulse to be a god herself.

Eve had the power to say no to the devil, she really did. Part of being made in God's image means being endowed with power. We have the ability to make decisions and choices. The Westminster Confession says, '[God] created man, male and female, with reasonable

and immortal souls, endued with knowledge, righteousness, and true holiness, after his own image; having
the law of God written in their hearts, and power to fulfil
it: and yet under a possibility of transgressing, being left
to the liberty of their own will.'[2] Two things mankind
is given at creation: power and possibility. The power to
obey, but the possibility to sin. Eve forsook her God-given
inner power, and went down the road of sin.

Once that happened, everything changed. In the
Fall, humanity forfeited the power to keep God's law.
Again, the Westminster Confession speaks so clearly
to this. In the chapter on free will we read: 'Man, by
his fall into a state of sin, hath wholly lost all ability
of will to any spiritual good accompanying salvation:
so as, a natural man, being altogether averse from that
good, and dead in sin, is not able, by his own strength,
to convert himself, or to prepare himself thereunto.'[3]
Augustine popularized the fourfold state of man. Before
the Fall, we were *able* to sin (*posse peccare*). Now we are
not able *not* to sin (*non posse non peccare*).

After the Fall, desires take over. Impulses and
cravings and lust rule the heart of man, overpowering
the ability to be spiritually disciplined. If we no longer
have that inner power, what are we? With no power,
no ability, we are nothing other than slaves to our lusts
and sinful desires. Paul says that the natural man is one

---

[2] Westminster Confession of Faith, 4.2.
[3] Westminster Confession of Faith, 9.3.

who lives 'in the passions of [their] flesh, carrying out
the desires of the body and the mind' (Eph. 2:3). Man
apart from God is obsessed with the world, which John
describes as being filled with 'the desires of the flesh and
the desires of the eyes and the pride of life,' and those
who are enslaved by those desires are 'passing away'
(1 John 2:16, 17).

Here we are learning why we need self-control so
badly: without it we cave to those sinful desires that
would have us careening towards hell. But the problem
is that, ever since Adam and Eve, we are unable to pull
the brake on those desires. We do not have that power
anymore.

How We Get It

So how do we get it? How do we get self-control, which is
so important? The answer is Jesus. Jesus is God's gracious
cure for the ruin brought to mankind by the Fall. So in
answering the question, *How do we get self-control?*, we
must begin in the life of Jesus.

The life of Jesus

Fast-forward from that tragic scene of temptation in the
garden to another scene of temptation, this time in the
wilderness. In a remarkably parallel fashion to Genesis
3, Matthew 4 portrays the devil coming once again to
God's chosen man on earth, trying to allure him to a life
of selfishness and sin. In this episode the devil tempts

Jesus three times, and notice something interesting about the first two: he wants Jesus to give a display of his power. 'Turn the stones to bread! Call your angels to save you from a daring stunt!' But Jesus never caves to Satan's taunts. He never gives him what he is after.

Is Jesus being weak here? Is this a sign of his impotence, a lack of power? Quite the opposite! This is the power of Christ on display—power over the prince of the power of the air, no less! Theologian Matthew Barrett, commenting on God's attribute of omnipotence, explains it like this:

> In a world in which *doing* things (doing everything) has become a sign of authority, we struggle to understand that there are situations in which *not doing something* is a far greater signifier of power … Jesus does not command stones to turn into bread—these non-acts display the greatest degree of power. To have done [this] would have been not powerful but weak, even sinful. Self-control is not a weakness but a sign that one is more powerful than those who cannot control themselves or their actions.[4]

There is another scene where we see Jesus display that self-control humanity lost at the Fall. It is, again, an astonishing parallel to Genesis 3. This time it takes place not in the Garden of Eden, but the Garden of Gethsemane. It is the moment of Jesus' betrayal and

---

[4] Matthew Barrett, *None Greater: The Undomesticated Attributes of God* (Grand Rapids, MI: Baker, 2018), p. 191.

arrest, with the crucifixion just hours away. Jesus is not tormented by a Tempter from without, like the devil in Matthew 4, but now he faces that inner struggle between his human desire and God's will. His human desire is, understandably, to shrink away from the thought of death, especially a death as gruelling as crucifixion. But he knows this is why he came. And so he prays, 'Father, if you are willing, remove this cup from me. Nevertheless, not my will, but yours, be done' (Luke 22:42). This is the prayer of self-control. Jesus recognizes something that would be an immediate good, namely, not having to endure the cross. But he is able to say, 'Your will be done, Father,' because in God's will he knows there is something much better guaranteed than relief from pain: there is redemption and glorification. Again, self-control is the ability to withhold a present desire in the confidence that something better is guaranteed in the future.

What would have happened if Jesus had no self-control? What if he had said, 'Father, let this cup pass from me. And if not, then I'm going to run.' What would have happened then? There would have been no cross. And with no cross, no death. And with no death, no grave. And with no grave, no resurrection. And with no resurrection, no hope. It is in no way an exaggeration to say we are saved because of the self-control of Jesus. We are saved by the One who came in our place and did the thing that God made us to do, but that we never did: he said 'No' to sin and to self.

The life of faith

The great thing about being a Christian is that you are not only saved from the sin of lacking self-control, you are also sanctified to be able to show self-control. When we have Jesus, we can start living life the way we were meant to live. That power that we forfeited in Eden is returned and restored to us: 'For the grace of God has appeared that brings salvation to all people. It teaches us to say "No" to ungodliness and worldly passions, and to live self-controlled, upright and godly lives in this present age' (Titus 2:11, 12, NIV). The true believer, endeavouring to live a life marked by faith, repentance, and the mortification of sin, knows how wonderful this word from Paul is: we can now say 'No' to sin. What good news!

But this can only come by faith in Jesus Christ. Remember, we are talking about the *fruit* of the Spirit. We only get that spiritual fruit by being connected to the Vine, which is Jesus himself. He says, 'I am the vine; you are the branches. Whoever abides in me and I in him, he it is that bears much fruit, for apart from me you can do nothing' (John 15:5). We need the life of Christ, and we need to respond to that in a life of faith. When we do that, we will begin to be sustained by the Vine, and begin to respond the way he responds to sin: not by conceding to it, but by conquering it. The life of faith will have the very power of the life of Christ.

Craig Troxel helpfully explains how the Christian can conquer sin:

Christ is constantly reshaping the will, not by removing its resolve but by reinforcing it. Christians are able to resist temptation by the power and grace that Christ the king supplies through his Spirit. He strengthens the will of our heart so that we will have toughness, assertiveness, and resilience when called for. Just as we are to set our hearts on him, he assures us that his heart is set on us, building up our hearts.[5]

Think again of the scene in Matthew 4. In every instance, Jesus responds with the word of God, proving that he is truly letting God's will and word control him. That is what self-control is, in the end. 'Self-control is ultimately the ability to be controlled, not by the sinful self, but by the Holy Spirit.'[6] What does verse 1 say? 'Then Jesus was led up *by the Spirit* ...' (emphasis added). Anointed by the Spirit, Jesus can respond to Satan's words with God's. Likewise, as he nears Calvary, as he struggles with inner turmoil, he finds inner power by turning to God in prayer. This is what we are to do as well. How do you respond to sinful urges and unwise impulses? The word of God and prayer must be your answer. Scripture and prayer are the sword and shield to mastering the sinful desires of self. Learn from Jesus himself!

Where is self-control most tested for you? Is it on the computer in the privacy of your room, or around the buffet at a party? Or perhaps it is your propensity to

---

[5] Troxel, *With All Your Heart*, pp. 137-138.
[6] Fesko, *The Fruit of the Spirit Is ...*, p. 57.

waste an entire Saturday 'binging' something on Netflix. Maybe it is on the treadmill, pushing yourself beyond your limitations. Maybe it is in the obsessive minutes you spend in front of the mirror. What does God's word say about these things? What does God hear you saying to him in prayer about these things? Are you convinced that God's plan is best, and that he will ultimately give us everything we need in his timing? Sinful desires demand an immediate response. The power of self-control is demonstrated in the one who has faith in this promise: 'The LORD is good to those who wait for him, to the soul who seeks him' (Lam. 3:25).

Be encouraged, dear believer: self-control is a wonderful gift that God gives us when we have the Spirit of Christ. 'For God gave us a spirit not of fear but of power and love and self-control,' Paul writes in 2 Timothy 1:7, again connecting the ideas of power and self-control. Or in Galatians 5:16, 'But I say, walk by the Spirit, and you will not gratify the desires of the flesh.' When you feel the powerful pull of sin, remember that you have a greater power. Our lapses into sin are instances where we neglect the Spirit of power within our very hearts. We must repent of these instances, and renew our desire to be strong in the Lord's strength.

The start of self-control is actually being controlled by Christ. 'If you would learn self-mastery, begin by yielding yourself to the One Great Master.'[7] The best use of your

---

[7] Jean Lobstein, quoted in *A Dictionary of Thoughts* (Detroit, MI: F. B. Dickerson, 1908), p. 510.

power is yielding it over to Jesus. It is in submitting to him and bowing the knee to him that we will find our greatest strength: 'Therefore, my beloved, as you have always obeyed, so now, not only as in my presence but much more in my absence, work out your own salvation with fear and trembling, for it is God who works in you, both to will and to work for his good pleasure' (Phil. 2:12, 13).

When you put your personal will on hold and let God's take precedence, even when it means waiting for good things that you want, it comes with the guarantee of gaining greater things that you need: joy, happiness, and heaven.

CONCLUSION:

BEAUTIFUL SAVIOUR, BEAUTIFUL SAINTS

My wife and I were once watching a documentary about forgeries of abstract expressionist paintings, purporting to be long-lost works of the likes of Mark Rothko and Jackson Pollock. Several aspects of the story bewildered us. First was the uncanny talent of these forgers to mimic the work of these artists so exactly. Second was the gift of the experts to spot the most minute and imperceptible details in order to distinguish the counterfeit from the original. But what bewildered us most of all was how these abstract expressionist pieces could easily be sold for millions and millions of dollars! It made no sense to us. What was so appealing about them? To us these works just looked like random shapes and squiggles on canvas—something I could have done in middle school art class and easily got an F for. And yet for many—for those who were more studied in the subject, who could view the pieces with the proper appreciation—these were near-priceless works of unparalleled beauty.

Is Jesus beautiful to you? This little book has aimed to put forth the unmatched beauty of Christ. It is something the world does not see or understand, and something we often miss as well. If Jesus is as unremarkable to you as some abstract brush strokes, then you are not viewing him through the proper lens. Scripture tells us that Jesus was not particularly physically attractive (Isa. 53:2), and yet his beauty shines forth from his character. Jonathan Edwards explains that the concept of virtue is nothing other than the resplendence of beauty in moral beings: 'Virtue is the beauty of the qualities and exercise of the heart, or those actions which proceed from them.'[1]

As we have considered these virtues from Galatians 5 in the life of Christ, we have been really considering the beauty of Christ. We have seen the sterling quality of his heart, and the actions that proceed from that heart. We have seen him love the loveless, feed the hungry, heal the lame, forgive the reprobate, be gentle towards the lowly. In all these ways, we share the astonishment of the crowds who remarked, 'He has done all things well' (Mark 7:37). Therein lies true beauty. In the person and work of Christ—a life that began in the squalor of a feeding trough and ended in the ignominy of public execution—all of the beauty and majesty that is God is made manifest.

[1] Jonathan Edwards, *A Dissertation Concerning the Nature of True Virtue*, in *Works*, 1:122.

Do you see it? Just like it takes the eye of the expert to appreciate a real Pollock, it takes the eye of faith to see the beauty of Christ. We see it in his loving mercy, his joyful determination, his peaceful disposition, his patient instruction, his kind and tender care, his good and right ways, his faithful commitment, his gentle invitations, and his execution of self-control to attain our salvation. And the wonderful thing is that when we take hold of this beautiful Saviour by faith, he will make us beautiful, too.

It starts gradually, but it does start now. Paul writes that 'we all, with unveiled face, beholding the glory of the Lord, are being transformed into the same image from one degree of glory to another' (2 Cor. 3:18). When we look *to* our Saviour we start to look *like* our Saviour. Paul goes on in that verse to explain how this is explicitly the work of the Holy Spirit: 'For this comes from the Lord who is the Spirit.' Jesus sends his Spirit to us to be the great Converter, the One who takes the dust that we are in Adam (Gen. 3:19) and converts it slowly but surely to the very glory of Christ.

Paul uses the word 'glory' here, and interestingly, in Exodus this is a word used in tandem with the attribute of beauty to describe the priests of Israel: 'Then bring near to you Aaron your brother, and his sons with him, from among the people of Israel, to serve me as priests— Aaron and Aaron's sons, Nadab and Abihu, Eleazar and Ithamar. And you shall make holy garments for Aaron your brother, *for glory and for beauty*' (Exod. 28:1, 2, emphasis added). The priests represented for the people what they were supposed to be, but what they could never attain on account of sin. We cannot hold a candle to the glory and beauty that God demands of us because of the stain of our transgressions. But what a relief to be found in Jesus:

> Jesus, thy blood and righteousness
> My *beauty* are, my *glorious* dress![2]

In my study hangs a poem by George Herbert entitled 'Aaron,' exquisitely rendered in calligraphy by one of my dear friends. Herbert is one of the greatest English poets of the seventeenth century. But he was also a pastor, a priest in the Church of England, and 'Aaron' is a poem for a pastor (though it has meaning for every Christian). The poem begins by describing the beauty of Aaron's priestly garb, as described in Exodus 28. Then it compares that with Herbert's own recognition that he is sinful, his heart falling far short of the beauty of the priest's outfit.

> Holiness on the head,
> Light and perfections on the breast,
> Harmonious bells below, raising the dead
> To lead them unto life and rest:
> Thus are true Aarons drest.

---

[2] Nikolaus Ludwig von Zinzendorf, trans. John Wesley, 'Jesus, Thy Blood and Righteousness', 1740 (emphasis added).

> Profaneness in my head,
> Defects and darkness in my breast,
>   A noise of passions ringing me for dead
> Unto a place where is no rest:
>   Poor priest, thus am I drest.

So what will Herbert do? What will any of us do when we recognize the defects and darkness that mark our heart? We put our hope in another heart:

> Only another head
> I have, another heart and breast,
>   Another music, making live, not dead,
> Without whom I could have no rest:
>   In him I am well drest.

> Christ is my only head,
> My alone-only heart and breast,
>   My only music, striking me ev'n dead,
> That to the old man I may rest,
>   And be in him new-drest.[3]

The Spirit *brings* us to the Great High Priest in order to *conform* us to him. God shows his love for us in not leaving us to the Devil's sway, which can only lead to dust and death, but rescuing us, regenerating us, and renovating us from the inside out. Whereas at one time we were conformed to the ugliness of the world, the Spirit conforms us to the glory of Christ (1 Pet. 1:14). Indeed, Owen was right to insist that the Spirit is 'the great beautifier of souls' who 'render[s] [us] by his grace all glorious within.'[4]

[3] George Herbert, 'Aaron', in *The Temple*, 1633.
[4] John Owen, *The Nature, Power, Deceit, and Prevalency of the*

Our doubts and our own continual failings in the Christian life would call this into question for many. When we look at photos of ourselves from years past, we can't ignore the evidence of decay and age in our bodies that has taken place since. There is no perceptible sign of renewal: just the opposite. We wonder, is the same thing happening with our souls? Writing in the 1700s, pastor and theologian John Brown of Haddington strikes confidence in the believer when he asks,

> If Satan mark his malice against us, and mark us his children, by introducing sinful habits, shall not God manifest his infinite love to us, in supernaturally implanting permanent habits or principles of holiness, as his permanent image on his children? Shall not Jesus Christ, by uniting his person, and imputing his righteousness to his members, and putting his Spirit with them, produce in them a permanent conformity to him, in the qualities of their heart?[5]

Don't you love the reiteration of the idea of permanence from Mr Brown? The Spirit permanently takes up residence in the hearts of true believers, which means the image of the very Son of God has been placed permanently upon us. Conformity to all of the beauty that is in Jesus *will* take place. The fruit of the Spirit is an inevitability for those who have the Spirit. Edwards writes with similar conviction:

Remainders of Indwelling Sin in Believers, in *Works*, 6:188.

[5] John Brown, *A Compendious View of Natural and Revealed Religion* (Grand Rapids, MI: Reformation Heritage Books, 2015), p. 406.

Christ is full of grace; and Christians all receive of his fulness, and grace for grace; *i.e.* there is grace in Christians *answering* to grace in Christ, such an answerableness as there is between the wax and the seal. There is character for character; such kind of graces, such a spirit and temper; the same things that belong to Christ's character belong to theirs. In that disposition wherein Christ's character in a special manner consists, does his image in a special manner consist … It would be strange if Christians should not be of the same temper and spirit with that of Christ; when they are *his flesh and his bone*, yea, are *one spirit*.[6]

If we have Christ, we have his character too. What a wonder. 'So we do not lose heart,' Paul tells us. 'Though our outer self is wasting away, our inner self is being renewed day by day' (2 Cor. 4:16). Do not permit your sin to tell you otherwise!

This is the truth we cling to until one day the renovation of the Spirit is complete. As we said in a previous study, the Spirit places heaven in us before he places us in heaven. But we *will* get there, and when we arrive the work will be complete. Vice will be entirely eradicated in our hearts. Virtue will flow freely from our affections to our actions. And why? John tells us: 'We know that when he appears we shall be like him, because we shall see him as he is' (1 John 3:2). Seeing Jesus by faith begins the work now, but seeing him in glory will

[6] Edwards, *Religious Affections*, in *Works*, 1:304.

complete it. We will become what we behold. It is no wonder that John Owen would give this exhortation: 'Let us live in the constant contemplation of the glory of Christ, and virtue will proceed from him to repair all our decays, to regrow a right spirit within us, and to cause us to abound in all duties of obedience.'[7]

So for now, dear Christian, behold the perfections of your Saviour in the inspired word. Let us begin now contemplating the glory of Christ, that vista that will occupy our sights for eternity. See his character. Learn of his heart. Worship his virtuous ways which won your salvation. And know that those graces that he so wonderfully exhibits, the Spirit has begun to form in your heart as well. Do this, and you will share the certainty of Paul: 'And I am sure of this, that he who began a good work in you will bring it to completion at the day of Jesus Christ' (Phil. 1:6).

———

[7] Owen, *Meditations and Discourses on the Glory of Christ*, in *Works*, 1:460.

FOR FURTHER STUDY
AND DISCUSSION

Introduction: This Is Not a How-To Book

1. Why do you think the fruit of the Spirit, as listed in Galatians 5, has been such a mainstay in Christian teaching over the centuries?

2. Have you experienced the temptation to view this list primarily in terms of what we must do for God, as opposed to what he will do for us? What is the practical significance of these two different approaches?

3. Explain the significance of the imagery of 'fruit' as traced throughout the Bible's storyline.

4. In what ways is the Spirit involved in the life and ministry of the Son? Why is this significant in terms of understanding the fruit of the Spirit?

5. What are the ways you can be drawn into a deeper love and a greater appreciation, wonder, and worship of the Lord Jesus Christ?

Chapter 1: The Love of God Made Manifest

1. How might you define love? How would this definition be similar or different from the ways a non-Christian might define it?

2. Why do the biblical writers seem to prize love above all other virtues? How might we do the same in our own lives?

3. This chapter listed several different types of love. Define them, and give examples of each in your own life.

4. The cross is the greatest expression of *agape*-love. Why?

5. God's love has been made manifest to us in the person of Jesus Christ (1 John 4:9)—how should you respond to such love? Bring in several scriptures to support your answer.

Chapter 2: The Joy of Your Master

1. What does the concept of joy make you think of? What people in your life would you characterize as joyful? Why?

2. John Piper said that Jesus 'is, and always will be, indestructibly happy.' What is your reaction to this statement?

3. What are the false sources of joy we often look to in life? Why are they so alluring, but ultimately so unsatisfying?

4. How could we ever heed Paul's command to 'rejoice in the Lord always' (Phil. 4:4)? Is this an impossibility? How do we square this call to joy with the inevitable hardships and trials of life?

5. How might you pursue joy at this stage of your life? What practices or habits do you need to change or establish?

Chapter 3: He Himself Is Our Peace

1. It was claimed in this chapter that 'peace' is one of the most important words in the entire Bible. In what sense, and do you agree? Give reasons for your answer.

2. What is reconciliation? What does it have to do with the concept of peace?

3. John Flavel said that we at times can be 'an enemy to our own peace.' Have you ever experienced that? How so?

4. What can we do to dispel doubt and anxiety and experience internal peace, such as Jesus experienced during the storm on the Sea of Galilee?

5. What are some common misconceptions of peace-making, and what is the biblical definition of it? Are you a peacemaker? What is the connection between the peace of Christ and the peace we can experience with one another?

Chapter 4: Consider Him Who Endured

1. What sorts of things test your patience?

2. Describe the difference and similarities between 'forbearance' and 'long-suffering.'

3. The weaknesses and sins of others call for our patient forbearance. How good are you at displaying that? Have you experienced this kind of patience from others? In what ways have you experienced forbearance from Christ?

4. In what ways does the patience of Christ call us to repentance?

5. What can we learn from the Scriptures about the long-suffering of Christ? In what ways might you be called to be long-suffering at this stage in your life?

Chapter 5: When Kindness Appeared

1. How do you define kindness? Are there specific examples of it that come to mind?

2. How does the world view kindness? Why do you think it is such a popular notion today?

3. What does kindness have to do with the character of God?

4. This chapter provided three scenes that show the kindness of Christ. In keeping with your definition given above, what other scenes could we add to that?

5. What impact could your display of Christ-inspired kindness have on those around you? In what ways might you be able to display it in the days ahead?

Chapter 6: 'Why Do You Call Me Good?'

1. Many theologians place goodness at the very centre of God's being. Why? What is the practical significance of understanding God in this light?

2. In what sense was the world made 'good'? Has sin entirely marred that goodness? In other words, can we still experience the goodness of God in the world today? If so, how?

3. Have you ever questioned the goodness of God? If so, in what situation?

4. Evaluate this common statement in light of the cross: 'Why would a good God allow bad things to happen to good people?'

5. In Romans Paul writes, 'For I do not do the good I want, but the evil I do not want is what I keep on doing' (7:19). What is the gospel's answer when we despair of a lack of goodness in our lives?

Chapter 7: Faithful to Him Who Appointed Him

1. Is there someone in your life that you would characterize as 'faithful'? What is it about them that causes this virtue to stand out? Perhaps more often you have

experienced the unfaithfulness of others (see Prov. 20:6)—what should you do in such situations?

2. Jesus is faithfulness incarnate primarily because he was faithful to his Father. In what ways do we see this faithfulness in the Gospels?

3. In his dying moments, J. Gresham Machen famously wrote, 'I'm so thankful for the active obedience of Christ: no hope without it.' Why should this faithful obedience of Christ be such a comfort to the Christian in death?

4. God's faithfulness to us is not contingent on our faithfulness to him (2 Tim. 2:13). Why is this good news, and how should we respond to it practically?

5. In what areas of faithfulness do you need to grow? Are you faithful to God? Are you faithful to your family? Are you faithful to your church? If you picked one aspect of life in which to become more reliable and committed, what would it be?

Chapter 8: Gentle and Lowly

1. What does it mean for God to deal with us gently? How have you experienced that in your life?

2. What does it mean that Jesus is 'lowly'? See Philippians 2:5-8 and Hebrews 4:15.

3. In what ways have you experienced the harshness and cruelty of the world? How did you respond or react at the time?

4. The call to exhibit this fruit of the Spirit challenges our pride. In what ways do you see your pride, and how might that change? (Remember from the chapter: the imperative comes only after the invitation!)

5. 'The heights of heaven cannot change the heart of Jesus which is set upon the lowly.' How might you explain the beauty of this truth to someone who is struggling with assurance?

Chapter 9: 'Not My Will but Yours Be Done'

1. What is the difference between trying to control our circumstances and trying to control ourselves? Which do you spend more time pursuing?

2. In what way is self-control 'power'? Does this comport with the modern concept of self-control?

3. Why is self-control a necessity in a fallen world?

4. What is the significance of the self-control of Jesus, especially as it was displayed at the Garden of Gethsemane?

5. Be encouraged to know that God's Spirit does give you the ability to exercise self-control. Reflect on passages such as Galatians 5:16, 2 Timothy 1:7, and Titus 2:11, 12. Have you experienced victory over particular sins in your life? What practical steps might you need to take to achieve greater victory and manifest this spiritual fruit in richer ways?

BANNER
of TRUTH

The Banner of Truth Trust originated in 1957 in London. The founders believed that much of the best literature of historic Christianity had been allowed to fall into oblivion and that, under God, its recovery could well lead not only to a strengthening of the church, but to true revival.

Interdenominational in vision, this publishing work is now international, and our lists include a number of contemporary authors, together with classics from the past. The translation of these books into many languages is encouraged.

A monthly magazine, *The Banner of Truth*, is also published, and further information about this, and all our other publications, may be found on our website, banneroftruth.org, or by contacting the offices below:

Head Office:
3 Murrayfield Road
Edinburgh
EH12 6EL
United Kingdom
Email: info@banneroftruth.co.uk

North America Office:
610 Alexander Spring Road
Carlisle, PA 17015
United States of America
Email: info@banneroftruth.org